THE BARE BONES OF
ADVERTISING PRINT DESIGN

THE BARE BONES OF ADVERTISING PRINT DESIGN

Robyn Blakeman

ROWMAN & LITTLEFIELD PUBLISHERS, INC.
Lanham • Boulder • New York • Toronto • Oxford

ROWMAN & LITTLEFIELD PUBLISHERS, INC.

Published in the United States of America
by Rowman & Littlefield Publishers, Inc.
A wholly owned subsidary of The Rowman & Littlefield Publishing Group, Inc.
4501 Forbes Boulevard, Suite 200, Lanham, MD 20706
www.rowmanlittlefield.com

P.O. Box 317, Oxford OX2 9RU, UK

British Library Cataloguing in Publication Information Available

Library of Congress Cataloging-in-Publication Data

Blakeman, Robyn, 1958–
    The bare bones of advertising print design / Robyn Blakeman.
        p.   cm.
    Includes bibliographical references and index.
    ISBN 0-7425-2961-4 (cloth : alk. paper)—ISBN 0-7425-2962-2
    (pbk. : alk. paper)
    1. Graphic design (Typography)   2. Advertising layout and design.
3. Newspaper layout and design.   4. Magazine design.   I. Title.

Z246.B56   2005
686.2'2—dc22

                                                                2005008244

Printed in the United States of America

∞ ™ The paper used in this publication meets the minimum
requirements of American National Standard for Information
Sciences—Permanence of Paper for Printed Library Materials, ANSI/
NISO Z39.48-1992.

CONTENTS

INTRODUCTION

This guide was written as a support for lecture and to give students studying newspaper and magazine design a few rules of thumb. Its purpose is not to give commands handed down from the mount, but a place to start building a strong design foundation.

I often thank the powers that be that you'll never get any two designers to agree on any one thing, let alone a rule or specific style. As a designer you have to grow and evolve, and to do that, you need a solid design foundation. Once you know the way and understand the why, you can then begin to explore the neighborhood on your own.

This guide will introduce you to the layout of the neighborhood where you plan to make a living, pointing out where the bullies and pit bulls live. Once you know the dangers, you can then begin exploring on your own, learning whose yards you can safely cut through and whose you cannot. Getting to your design destination in one piece is the only absolute governing design.

The basic rules of design exist for all of us; it's what you do with them that will matter. Once you've worked with them for a while, you will throw out those you find inhibiting, unnecessary, or limiting and develop the others into your own personal creative style.

CHAPTER ONE

DESIGN AND THE ADVERTISING PROCESS

THE BUSINESS OF CREATIVITY

Creative doesn't just happen; it's the result of months of research, planning, and preparation. When it's time to develop an idea, your direction will be based on a multiphase business plan started months earlier.

Young designers often believe they get to do anything they want creatively. Nothing could be further from the truth. Budget and a client's marketing initiatives most often hinder creativity. You do not design for yourself; you design to sell a product or service to a predetermined set of individuals or **target market.**

Most of us think of advertising as the creative product; that's probably what first attracted you to advertising as a career path. However, the creative aspect is only one small portion of the process of advertising. Advertising is a business first and a creative outlet second.

The road to effective creative is well defined. It begins with the research of the product or service, competition, and target and moves on to the development of a marketing plan, a creative strategy, and finally a creative brief. Let's take a very brief look at each one.

RESEARCH

The organization of research takes place in the marketing plan. Research can be qualitative or quantitative in nature. **Qualitative data** employs the use of open-ended questions that can be distributed and collected through interviews or convenience polling. Focus groups are another frequently used option. A **focus group** gathers together a representative sample of the target, usually ten to twelve people, to use or try the product in a controlled environment.

Quantitative data, on the other hand, is comprised of closed-ended or controlled surveys, where participants must choose their answers from a preselected set of responses. Surveys can be conducted over the phone, at the mall, or from panel studies.

The type of research gathered will depend on projected outcomes and the product or service to be advertised. It will also depend on who will be using the product or service.

TARGET MARKET

Your **target market** consists of those individuals who have been determined most likely to buy your product or use your service. When determining a target market, you will look at several personal attributes.

Isolating Target Attributes

The more you know about who will be using your product, the better you can target your message directly to them. Personal attributes of the target are known as **demographics,** which includes sex, age, income, marital and professional status, education, and number of children, to name just a few. Your target can be broken down further to include **psychographics,** or lifestyle, and **geographics,** or where a person lives. Good ideas should talk to the target in words they can understand. To do this effectively, we have to isolate target attributes in a more personalized way. Within your target are two very distinct ways of thinking.

Left Brain versus Right Brain: A Thought

By understanding how the consumer thinks, acts, and feels, we can more accurately target our communication message to meet their needs. These needs are controlled by the brain, which is divided into two halves, the left side and the right side.

The left side of the brain controls reading and verbal skills, as well as the logical and rational thought processes that make an individual's outlook more conservative. This is the side that tells you not to step out in front of a moving vehicle, and that you need a parachute when jumping from an airplane.

The left side of the brain is also responsible for your math skills as well as your ability to memorize facts, names, and vocabulary.

The right side of the brain is the more passive, liberal, emotional, and visual side. Its strengths include a vivid imagination, musical abilities, and a more open-minded or liberal outlook. The right-brained person needs to see a message repeatedly, in multiple forms of media, before reacting to that message. The more active or left-brained individual will often respond to a message by researching a product or service more thoroughly through customer service calls and annual or consumer reports, or by surfing the Web.

Most of us use a little of the abilities from both sides of our brain. We avoid that moving car; we love music or books, but hate math.

It is critical that these left- and right-brained attributes be taken into consideration when creating visual/verbal relationships in advertising design. A left-brained individual relies on facts to make a decision, making copy more important. The more right-brained individual relies more on the visual aspects of the ad. The overall creative message needs to appeal to both kinds of individuals within our target market.

Initially, the basic needs for each of these individuals differ. If for example, you are advertising a car, the left-brained consumer will be more interested in facts such as gas mileage and safety features, whereas the right-brained consumer will be more interested in seeing the car and knowing about color choices rather than engine size. It's not that right-brainers don't care about safety or that left-brainers don't care about what the car looks like; they're just not the first or most important things they consider.

One way to create a strong visual/verbal relationship that immediately attracts the attention of both learners is to have a strong headline explaining a consumer benefit, accompanied by an answering visual. In other words, attract the left-brainer with words and the right-brainer with pictures. Another option is to attract the right-brainer with copy that paints a visual picture of them experiencing the car; this will also work for the left-brainer if you intersperse relevant facts within the visual copy. This type of approach is particularly important for new product introductions, additions, and/or upgrades.

The more knowledge you have about your product, client, target, and competition, the more ammunition you have for creative ingenuity. The foundation for creative ideas is laid out in a document known as a marketing plan.

MARKETING PLAN

A **marketing plan** is your client's business plan. It outlines the company's strengths and weaknesses as well as the opportunities and threats affecting the product or service. A marketing plan determines marketing objectives, or what is to be accomplished; it profiles the marketing strategy, or how objectives will be met; and it looks at budget issues and evaluation tactics.

CREATIVE STRATEGY

The **creative strategy** is an integral part of the marketing process. Once we know the marketing goals set up by our client, we can begin developing an effective creative strategy that will accomplish them. Effective strategies are the slippery yet essential monsters that define advertising direction. You are not looking at ideas yet, but at solution(s) to an advertising problem. These solutions assist in the development of a concept or theme that can consistently be executed within multiple media without losing substance or focus.

A creative strategy is the harness needed to direct the power and effectiveness of ideas. It is your communications plan of attack.

The overall interpretation of the creative strategy by the creative team begins the construction phase of message development.

CREATIVE BRIEF

The **creative brief,** or **copy platform,** is developed from the creative strategy and defines your big idea or unique selling proposition (USP). Additionally, the creative brief looks at individual features and consumer benefits associated with your product or service, outlines tactics, and redefines the target market.

Creatives—that is, art directors and/or copywriters—often use the creative brief during concept development. It is a detailed map that outlines the product or service and keeps the creative team on strategy, or accomplishing the creative or strategic goals.

A Unique but Big Selling Idea

Creatives begin the conceptual process by examining the ad's overall strategy or focus. This focus can be executed via either a unique selling proposition (USP) or a big idea. The approach you choose is determined by a product's individual features and benefits and an art director's creative imagination. To determine which approach to use, you must look at your product or service and decide what makes it special: Which product or service feature is screaming creative stardom?

- A **unique selling proposition (USP)** is used when a consumer benefit is offered that is unique to your client's product or service. USPs are also used in promoting a commonplace feature as unique.
- A **big idea** is a creative solution that sets your product off from the competition while at the same time solving a client's advertising problem. This does not mean the competition does not have the identical feature(s), only that they are not pushing it in their advertising. When using a big idea, creativity is the key to success.

Expressing Your USP or Big Idea

Every ad has a style or personality assigned to it by the designer. How it's expressed depends on the approach, or tone of voice used to communicate the USP or big idea. Ask yourself what kind of image this product or service should project. Can that image be developed through emotion, humor, or a fact-based approach? Is it newsworthy, or should a specific feature be promoted? Should you remind or tease your target, or will a demonstration or instructional approach do the trick? Whichever approach you take, it should work toward building up the brand's image and successfully promoting your USP or big idea.

The **emotional approach** works on a consumer's needs and wants. How will they look or feel using the product; how does it stimulate the senses? The sell is made by creating a scenario into which consumers can place themselves. Facts about a product are not as important as the image and personal satisfaction the product will bring. This approach works well when there are few differences setting your product off from the competition.

A **humorous approach** looks at the product and the target and places all in an unusual or outrageous situation in which the product solves a problem.

A **factual approach** works on a consumer's needs and wants as well; but instead of selling to the emotions or imagination, you make your sell based only on the facts associated with the product. This approach relies heavily on the benefits and features of the product or service.

News event or **educational approaches** are used when your product is in the news. Perhaps your client or the product has won an award for quality or service. Being first at anything is not only newsworthy, but a great sales approach.

A **feature approach** concentrates on one major feature of your product. It would be nice if it were unique to your product; but even an appliance's plug can be made unique if your competition is not pushing plugs, and your concept is unique and memorable.

The **reminder approach** keeps well-known products such as common salt or seasonal products in the mind of the consumer.

A **teaser approach** is used to create interest in a product that is not yet on the market. This approach should build curiosity and entice the consumer by talking about a product but not showing it.

Using a **demonstration approach** compares your product to the competition; each product's strengths and weaknesses are weighed.

An **instructional approach,** as its name implies, teaches the consumer how to do something or how your product or service can solve a problem.

Additional approaches might compare your product to the competition or create a spokesman or animated personality, creating a personalized approach to your advertising. You can never go wrong with a testimonial or endorsement. In a **testimonial,** a celebrity or common man on the street endorses your product by telling their personal experiences with the product. **Endorsements** are a little different; the announcer or celebrity does not personally use the product and is being paid for their time.

SELLING THE PRODUCT'S FEATURES AND BENEFITS

One mistake young designers often make is to sell a product's features and not its benefits. Before making a purchase, every person in the target market wants to know what's in it for them. Let's use a toaster as an example.

Feature: It comes in five different colors.

Benefit: Makes coordination with your kitchen color theme easier.

Feature: Comes in two-, four-, or six-slice models.

Benefit: No matter what size of family you have to feed, there is a toaster size that makes it faster and easier.

Features are lovely, but they have no point. The point that needs to be hammered home is what the feature can offer the consumer. Determining a benefit for each of your product's features helps break down the product information into smaller, more manageable bundles, giving concept development a visual/verbal starting point.

WHERE DOES A GOOD IDEA ORIGINATE?

All great ads begin with a good idea. A good idea can come from an overactive imagination, pain, observation, experience, or just plain luck. It is the thing that drives concept. All good designers need to be culturally diverse, stay open-minded, and have an overactive imagination. This realm of endless possibilities, this dream state, is the place to define and build ideas. Go beyond the MTV culture and look at the world as it was and as it is. What *was* is very important in defining what is.

Go outside your immediate likes and dislikes. Start with music, and experience new sounds like those from the archives of rock, jazz, blues, or country western. Music is a powerful weapon; everyone relates to it in one way or another. Music makes listeners active participants, whether they're reminiscing or singing along.

Next, go to museums and art galleries to see how art, like advertising, marks history and defines cultures and attitudes. Attend independent film festivals, another cultural marker; note how your peers speak and represent culture both past and present. Go to the park or the mall and people-watch; play with a child; talk to the elderly. Don't define or label anything you see; just experience it. After all, if we want our advertising to touch a reader's, viewer's, or listener's taste buds or fashion consciousness, we need to understand their world.

Readers and viewers alike respond to stimulants—whether they remind them of something from their childhood or college days or of something they haven't yet experienced, but wish to. If you plant the thought, the consumer will decide whether or not to experience your idea.

Your imaginative thoughts will eventually lay the groundwork for an idea. That idea will need to be developed into a concept direction for your client's product or service.

All great ads begin by developing, producing, and then eliminating hundreds of ideas that just didn't measure up. Open your conservative mind, and your liberal imagination will follow.

Daydreaming and role-playing are a designer's first line of defense when struggling to solve a client's advertising problem, and they are actually an important part of the design process. Those carefree dreams acted out in the backyard—when you imagined yourself a pilot, astronaut, explorer, princess, clown, or juggler—are just waiting to be resurrected. Feel free to act up and act out. Jump aboard that broomstick horse; rebuild that impenetrable fort made of boxes, sticks, and whatever was left over from

Mom and Dad's last home improvement idea. Or better yet, run outside or look out the window, and excavate that passing cloud for a recognizable image. As an adult, you'll find these are the kinds of thoughts and acts that inspire award-winning ads and memorable slogans.

All that said, the problem is that most of us have had imagination beat out of us in the formative years of our schooling—the years when our imagination is the most active and inventive. Reignite your imagination, and pump up your dreams—because creativity requires a bizarre and innovative thinker, a trendsetter and fad developer.

It's time to reacquaint yourself with your inner child. Instead of feeling ridiculous acting out your innermost creative thoughts, feel inspired.

CHAPTER TWO

THE MAIN INGREDIENT TO GREAT DESIGN

Indulge in the Tastiness

Slim•Fast Recipes

THE CREATIVE PROCESS

There is a lot of bad advertising out there with no direction, no strong brand identity, and no defined target market. This kind of advertising usually carries what I call a "been there, done that" creative label. That means the idea was often stolen from another product. How many times do consumers have to see creative teams blow up, or animate, the Statue of Liberty—or worse yet, make the Mona Lisa smile—for yet another product? When you've seen something once, it's interesting; when you've seen it two or three times, it's boring. Once consumers are bored, they're no longer paying attention to the message.

Today's consumer is bombarded with hundreds of advertising messages. A good creative recognizes this and looks for an innovative way to make their product stand out among the clutter. Budweiser did it with the "wassup" campaign, and Energizer did it with the "pink bunny" campaign.

Coming up with that extraordinary idea is not as easy as most people think it is. It involves using both sides of the brain effectively. As the left

Quickly rendered thumbnails should highlight concept skills.

side sorts out all the research you've collected, the right side begins the imagination process.

An active imagination is commendable, but it is fallible, and not every idea will be a good idea. However, believing your ideas are the best ideas is the only way to approach the creative process. Fortunately—or unfortunately, depending on how you look at it—there is always someone around to deny or confirm our brilliance. To help define brilliance, creatives often work in teams.

The creative team is made up of an art director(s)—a visual right-brainer—and one or more copywriters, the verbal left-brainers. They're responsible for developing the big idea, writing ad copy, and designing ads that bring the big idea or unique selling proposition (USP) to life. The creative team takes these ideas and matches them to each media vehicle's strengths and limitations. When left- and right-brained people work together, visual and verbal communication become a powerful problem-solving combination.

WHO ARE THE CREATIVES?

Creative, as used in this text, is a broad term for the conceptual process. A **creative** is a person who is involved in creative activity, especially involving the creation of advertisements. *Creative* can also refer to the advertising material that is produced by **creatives.** The creative team is comprised of some very eclectic personalities. Job titles, which are as diverse as the personalities that fill them, depend on where you are in the country and on the size of the agency. I will talk here only about the most common and generally accepted titles.

> *Creative director.* This title probably varies most across the country, but basically this person is the boss or team leader. He or she handles administrative and/or management functions and is most often involved with television or high-profile projects.
> *Art director.* Job titles range from junior through senior levels. Art directors are the workhorses of the advertising agency; they have their hands in everything. On any given day they could be working on newspaper, magazine, point-of-purchase (POP) advertising, direct mail, or television. The person in this position needs to know a lot about the creative process, from conceptual development to photo shoots to production.
> *Copywriter.* These team members write copy, and like art directors, have a range of titles. Copywriters can find themselves writing copy

for multiple media vehicles and even more diverse types of products.

THE CREATIVE CONCEPT

What is it? **Creative concept** is an idea that imaginatively solves the client's advertising problem. Coming up with a brilliant and effective idea takes a lot of hard work. Before you can isolate one great idea, you must pursue many mediocre ones. Conceptual development or *brainstorming* is a process that starts when you kick your imagination into overdrive and expose the "unthought-of."

BRAINSTORMING

Brainstorming is your imagination at work. In the process, good ideas, partial ideas, and bad ideas are considered, developed further, or thrown out.

Brainstorming is still done the old-fashioned way—from gray cells to mouth to paper. Brainstorming sessions may be comprised of a creative team of copywriters and art directors, or they may involve a solitary session in which just you and your thoughts mature. Nothing is set in stone, apart from the product's features, so as not to limit the number of ideas the session may generate.

There is no specific way that creatives brainstorm ideas; the main goal is to discuss the product's features and imagine a way to present them. Within these features lies the product's inherent drama. What makes it tick? What aspects are interesting or unusual? How will it benefit the target market? Brainstorming isolates that benefit and places it within various scenarios that have meaning to your target market. The result should cause them to think. People don't pay attention to abstract ideas; they pay attention to realism, and they want to know how the product or service can solve their personal problem or need.

A traditional brainstorming session may begin with a copywriter throwing out a headline to promote the USP or big idea while the art director, with drawing pad and marker in hand, quickly roughs out a visual that supports the headline. On the average, a creative team can come up with anywhere from 50 to 100 ideas per session. Of course, not all of these ideas will be brilliant. Some ideas are weak, some too complicated, others just plain stupid; but each one inspires another direction or even the possible combination of ideas.

The next step? Search for quality in the quantity. Ideas with potential will eventually be reworked and narrowed down to three to five ideas or concepts that are presented to the client.

How Do I Know a Creative Idea When I Think of It?

Here's another one of those good questions: How do you know when you've thought of a creative idea? I will start by saying that if you've seen it done before, it's no longer creative. It's that "been there, done that" thing again. Once an idea becomes mainstream, the target's interest isn't held, as it would be with a new and innovative approach.

You will recognize a good idea when it comes along, basically because it doesn't stink as bad as the rest. It's also dead-on strategy, or meets the goals laid out in the marketing objectives.

Ideas can come from anywhere. You might witness something relevant on the street, or overhear a devastatingly good conversation on the bus or at the office coffeepot. Cocktail conversation is often enlightening, and nothing can compete with basic personal experience. Talk about it, think about it, question it, position it, brand it, place it in a relevant setting or even an irrelevant one, let it stand alone, compare it to the competition, show before-and-after results, twist it or bend it; but make it your own. When enlightenment finally does come—and it will come, trust me— pounce on it.

Enemies to Creativity

The biggest enemy to creativity is the lack of exploration. By that I mean you took shortcuts. You did not fully research both your client and the competition, so your ideas are off target or off strategy. Second, and per- haps most important, you did not experiment with multiple ideas that forced you to flex your brain's imagination muscles.

Most novice creatives believe that their first idea is their best idea. I'm here to tell you that you only think it's your best idea—because it's your only idea.

Great ideas take a lot of work, and once you think you've found a direction that will solve the client's problem, you'll do a lot of reworking to perfect it. Great concepts must be on target. In other words, the concept must speak to the target market in words they understand and relate to situations they find themselves in. Advertising that is off target or off strat- egy can be very entertaining, oftentimes even brilliant; but if it doesn't create sales and raise awareness, it's useless.

All ideas, good or bad, should begin with thumbnails.

Computers and Design: Putting It All Down on Paper

Computers and *design* are two words that should never appear together. Imagination is spontaneous and original; it is not about moving the same ideas around the screen or importing prepackaged photos or illustrations. The computer is a tool—not a solution for a good idea.

Your mind is still faster than a computer chip, and much more imaginative. Perhaps your hand skills will never catch up, but your mind and its spontaneity will never be surpassed. You never know when inspiration will strike. I can pretty much guarantee that brilliance won't wait for you to get home and boot up the computer. When ideas come, they explode in your head. The point is just to get them down on paper, whether visually or verbally, as soon as possible. Consider keeping a notepad near you at all times; you never know when a great idea may pop into your head. I keep one on the bedside table and one in the car because, unfortunately, some of my best ideas come while I'm sleeping or sitting in traffic. An overactive imagination should never get a good night's sleep. You don't want to lose a single idea if you can avoid it; so doodle, write, or even record it, but just get it down.

It is important to understand that the computer is a production device, not a design scapegoat. The computer cannot dream or imagine; it reproduces, period. Once the *idea* is solidified, then you can move it to the computer for finishing touches.

Imagination, emotion, and participation are what set us apart from machines in design. Our ability to see, feel, hear, taste–even daydream, as others in our species do—allows us to create or even exploit reality. So dream it in your head, see it come alive on paper, and reproduce it on the computer.

CHAPTER THREE

THE MANY STAGES OF DESIGN

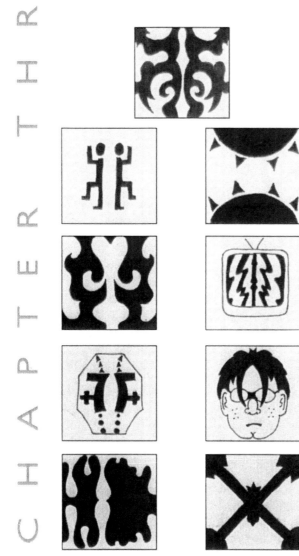

THE ELEMENTS AND PRINCIPLES OF DESIGN

Before you can develop that great idea, before you boot up the computer, you must first understand the rules that govern good design. The ability to tie together the components within an ad, creating harmony and structure on the page, is critical to creating an ad that flows, is cohesive, and a delight to the eye. The design should set a tone or pace for the consumer and be easy to read and understand. These basic rules are known as the principles and elements of design.

These guidelines for design lay the groundwork for understanding the look of design. They offer options for creative diversity. Anything goes when it comes to creative conceptual ideas; but when designing on the page, there are rules that help to make the design a success and message delivery easier to understand.

The Elements of Design

An element of design is an emotion or detail expressed through color or form. Designers can choose from many design elements, as described in the following paragraphs.

Color

Color, or the lack thereof, creates a mood. A design may use many colors or just one or two strategically placed. A brand's image can be defined through the use of color.

Line

Using lines in an ad should take the viewer's eye to a predetermined destination. Lines can be drawn or implied; straight, curved, or zigzagged; or they can be used to point out details.

Shape

Shape is used in design to break up the page. Most shapes are one-dimensional or flat. Using shadow can give a flat shape a three-dimensional appearance.

Shapes can be geometric or organic. *Geometric* shapes include circles, squares, rectangles, triangles, and lines. Most components in an ad will reflect one or more of the preceding shapes. *Organic* shapes are those shapes found in nature that do not fit the geometric mold.

Any shape can be filled or surrounded by type or color. The inherent knowledge that circles are smooth and triangles are sharp can create specific emotions.

Texture

Texture can be created by using lights and darks as well as by grouping repetitive shapes such as lines or triangles. Texture can also be depicted by using known objects or shapes—shards of glass, pebbles, carpet, or steel wool. Using texture as a design tool should encourage viewers to run their hand over the ad, or relate to their personal experience of how ticklish a feather can be.

Value

Value highlights details or textures through the use of lights and darks. Value creates the illusion of distance. Objects that are close to the viewer will seem larger, darker, and richer in color. Textures will be more detailed. Objects appearing in the distance will be smaller and more muted in color and have little or no defined texture.

Offering the viewer varied values creates interest in specific areas within a photograph or illustration. Not everything in a photograph or illustration is of equal importance. The darkest or most colorful areas will attract the viewer's eye first. For example, people often look at another person's eyes first. If you want the viewer to notice the teeth first, then darken the face; the teeth will then look whiter. Light is happy; dark is dreamy or dramatic. Use value to create moods, depth, or texture.

Volume

Adding volume to a product gives it a three-dimensional appeal. By adding shadows, you can make an object appear to have depth. You can also give the illusion of volume by extending a portion of an object beyond a border. This could be accomplished by placing a border around a small inset photograph; a portion of the figure within the photograph could extend beyond or over the border. This also gives the appearance of movement in shape and form.

The Principles of Design

The principles of design should be considered as the rules for good design. In the following paragraphs, you'll learn the basic principles at work in an

Properly placed elements in this asymmetrical
design create balance.

effective ad. By incorporating one or more of the principles or elements
in any ad, you will help the design flow and visually assist the reader
through the ad.

Balance

An ad is in balance when all of its components appear to have equal
weight. When too many components are placed on one side or another,
the ad looks like it is about to tip over. When too much weight is placed
at the top, the ad appears to squish the smaller elements at the bottom.

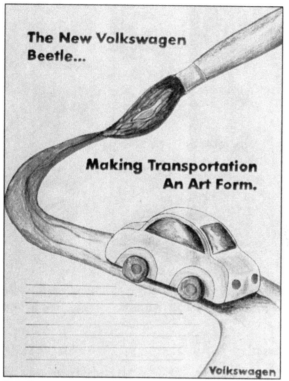

Eye flow leads the reader on an informational
adventure.

Eye Flow

The principle of eye flow involves aligning the ad components so the eye
can follow a predetermined path through the ad. It is important for all
components to be read and seen in the proper order. All designs should
move the eye from left to right and from top to bottom easily. Instead of
telling viewers where to go within the ad, show them by creating a trail of
components that flows from the opening headline or visual to the closing
logo or slogan.

Asymmetrical Design

The asymmetrical design principle sees an ad as having two sides, evenly
divided by an imaginary line. Objects within the ad appear to be dispro-
portionately placed on either side of this imaginary line. Usually the components of an ad are not of equal weight, size, or number. To counter the

Asymmetrical examples.

unbalanced look and to create a balanced look within, the ad's components must be arranged or grouped so that both sides appear to be balanced.

Symmetrical Design

As in asymmetrical design, the symmetrical design principle appears to divide an ad down the middle. The main difference is that the components appearing on either side of the ad are identical in weight, number, and size. This design is great for comparing various qualities, or presenting "both sides" of a product.

Structure

The principle of structure represents control over the design. Placement of each component has a controlled or thought-out appearance. Nothing is randomly placed; layout qualities are consistent. When designing, for example, if all components within the ad are centered, placing a subhead in the middle that is set flush left goes against the ad's structure. Everything has a purpose. Purpose can be created through repetition of layout qualities.

Repetition

The design principle of repetition is used to create a pattern or movement. Same-shape elements are arranged to show a relationship. Movement can be created by slightly overlapping same-shape elements that grow in size

Symmetrical examples.

or move from light to dark. This works great for showing growth or change.

Anomaly

An anomaly is the misfit within an orderly pattern. When you want your product to stand out from the crowd of similar products, consider creating a pattern of like products. Your product is placed within the pattern, showing its uniqueness among the masses. Do not place your product in the center; place it closer to the headline or logo, making it easier for viewers to remember the name among the crowd.

Concentration

The design principle of concentration shows movement. If you were to spill a glass of water or dump over a salt shaker, the contents would spread

An anomaly layout focuses on how your
product is different from the competition.

across the page at random. The eye will follow the flow or spill to a speci-
fied point—that is, copy, product, or logo.

Dominance

One item in *every* design should stand out, or dominate the page. This
should be the first thing the eye notices in a design. The item can be either
a visual element or a headline. One large visual, or a group of multiple
visual elements, can create a dominant visual image. A headline in a very
large or bold typeface is a great way to scream a consumer benefit.

Gradation

Gradation reflects the qualities of a sunset. It can be accomplished with
color or stages of gray or through the use of thick to thin lines or large to

Repetition. This example shows movement
through size changes.

small shapes. Stacking small and large shapes on top of one another creates weight or even instability. Add a dark color or tones, and the instability is magnified. Gradation of tones or colors can show movement,
distance, shadows, or highlights.

Contrast

Items can be differentiated based on size, value, tone, color, shape, or
texture. Using the design principle of contrast is a great way to make
similar items placed together appear unique or independent.

Harmony

Through the principle of harmony, the elements within a design work together to create a coherent message. In advertising design, this means the
copy has a relationship with the visual(s).

Negative/Positive Space

The design principle of negative/positive space works a little differently
when used in advertising than when used purely as a design element. In

Anomaly examples.

advertising, we see negative space as the white of the paper or unused space; the positive space, or black portion, is the text and/or visuals appearing within an ad.

Positive space in printing is just the opposite. When negatives are pulled during the printing stage, the occupied space is clear and the unoccupied space is black. Light can pass through the clear areas of the negative, reproducing the ad. The negative's black areas do not allow light to pass through, protecting the white of the page.

Radiation

Used more often in graphic design than advertising design, the principle of radiation shows movement. Geometric shapes and strong blacks and

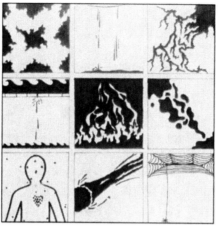

Concentration examples.

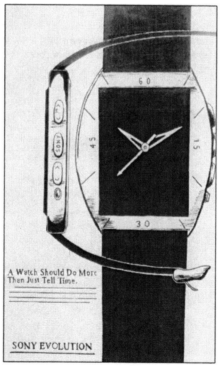

Dominance. Creating a dominant focal point takes the reader immediately to the most important point in the design.

Gradation. Tonal changes can create movement throughout an ad and take the reader on a journey.

Contrast.

Harmony. This visual/verbal relationship
works because it uses a play on words to tie
the contrasting visuals to the headline copy.

whites give the images the illusion of movement—like heat radiating off
hot pavement.

Unity

The principle of unity requires that all elements within the ad have a relationship to one another.

THE STAGES OF DESIGN

In this section, we'll look at four stages of the design process: concept,
thumbnails, roughs, and super comprehensives.

Concept

The first stage in the design process is brainstorming or concept development. **Creative concept** refers to your thoughts and ideas on how you can

Unity. Comfort by example, both visually and verbally, gives this ad a purpose.

creatively solve the client's advertising problem. Concept sets the tone and direction for a single ad or a combination of ads. This is where bad ideas come to die, and good ideas get a second look and perhaps an overhaul and face-lift. It's also where daydreams begin to see the light of day. Here the creative team hammers out sometimes hundreds of ideas, only ten percent of which will bear further development.

All those daydreams come out as ideas, though many of them will be rejected. Others may stand the test of development, and all are worth sharing. It is important when you have an idea to present it to others, whether they're other professionals or your classmates. Don't worry about whether your ideas are stupid. I guarantee that you will excel in the realm of the ridiculous; you will be teased, and you may never live it down, but you will inspire ideas in others by sharing your not-so-fabulous thoughts as well as those brilliant ones.

Word Lists

The best place to start when trying to develop a great idea is to begin with what I refer to as a word list. A word list gets your left and right brain working. Believe it or not, there are multiple ideas amid your gray matter; you just need to get them out of there and into reality. It's also important to realize that great ideas, for the most part, do not just pop into your head. They will most likely come in bits and pieces, such as in a word list, that comes together at the most unlikely of times and places—in a business meeting, the subway, or the shower.

A word list starts the brainstorming process. This is the best way to experience how consumers think; at the same time, it helps build your conceptual skills. A word list is composed of three columns or parts.

The left or first column represents the left brain. Here is where you list the facts about your product or service; let's use an orange.

Fact Column One: Orange
                  Round
                  Sour
                  Slice

In the second or middle column, choose a descriptive or visual word(s) to represent the product/service fact used in column one (a thesaurus works great for assistance with column two). This column should lead to previously "unthought-of" directions. Here is where "been there, done that" goes to die.

Fact Column Two: Sunshine
                  Navel
                  Face Contortion
                  Saw
                  Knife
                  Teeth

The third or right column is where you describe how the combinations of these two words might be used in an ad. Ask yourself questions. Consider the five W's—Who, What, When, Where, Why—and don't forget How. Create a scenario for use either visually or verbally.

Fact Column Three: HOT, HOT, HOT, TASTE.
                    Show a human navel, talk about connection to Mother Earth.
                    Show varied people's reaction to their first bite of an orange.
                    No matter how you slice it . . . show the options being used on an orange.

The third column, representing right-brain traits, should create something we can feel, taste, or just genuinely experience. Set up your word list so the words are aligned across the page from left to right; one or more ideas can be expressed in any column for any word.

1. Orange	Sunshine	HOT, HOT, HOT, TASTE.
2. Round	Navel	Show a human navel, talk about the connection to Mother Earth.
3. Sour	Face Contortion	Show varied people's reaction to their first bite of an orange.
4. Slice	Saw Knife Teeth	No matter how you slice it . . . Show the options being used on an orange.

Now you try it. What product or service do these words impart to you?

1. Safety	Tranquil	(How would you describe it?)

Remember, a good ad should contain elements needed for both left- and right-brain consumers.

Are Word Lists Really Useful?

Why do a word list? It opens up your imagination and teaches you to think visually and relate verbally. Word lists help you reinvent your imagination while at the same time building your word power. This is a way to communicate to both sides of your consumers' brain. A good word list should include 20–25 words and visual representations.

The goal of all creative is to develop an image or express an idea that is unique to your client. "Been there, done that" creative is eliminated when you explore your infinite options. That means conservative views must sometimes step aside and let the liberal ideas step up. For instance, how many of you would have chosen a duck to sell insurance or used Frankenstein to sell joint cream? How many of you would have chosen instead to use a pitchman talking about protecting your family or show a bunch of athletes sitting around talking about pain? Exercising your infinite options really puts a new spin on "never been there, never done that," doesn't it?

Breaking concept ideas down to one or two words helps you to focus on the point you're trying to solve. One way to break out of been there, done that—the conservative approach to advertising syndrome—is to create and live a little inside your word list.

Thumbnails

Thumbnails, or **thumbs,** are the second stage in the design process. Word lists play an important role in thumbnail development. Ideas generated there become a reality at this stage.

Thumbnails are small proportionate drawings, ranging in size from $2 \times 3\frac{1}{2}$ inches to 3×5 inches, that are used to place your concept ideas on paper. Each thumbnail idea should reflect a different concept direction, headline, subhead, and visual; no two should be alike. Try to use a different layout style for each concept. Further development should inspire alternative concept approaches.

The word *doodle* best describes what a thumbnail should look like. Random headlines, visuals, and layout styles should offer varied solutions to further develop your concept.

Thumbnails can have any number of combinations and components, but usually will consist of one or more of the following: a readable headline and possible subhead(s), a recognizable visual(s), body copy indication, and a logo. Each thumb should be enclosed in a box, representing the

Offer your client variety by creating as many different headlines to express your USP or big idea as possible.

Sometimes your visuals need to shine and your copy
needs to shout.

final size and shape of the ad, and should be tightly drawn and consistent
in size.

Thumbs should be done in black marker. Color may be added when
working within a color medium such as magazine. Right off the bat, get
into the habit of working in marker. Avoid pencils. Markers allow you to
work and rework without the benefit of an eraser. When you can erase,
you can obsess on one thumbnail idea. If you make a mistake or just don't
like the way the idea is going, cross it out and move on; that's erasing,
designer style.

Clients do not usually see thumbnails; but for students, good, clean,
well-designed thumbs can go directly into a thumbnail book for presentation in your portfolio. Headlines, subheads, slogans, and logos should be
written out cleanly and placed in position on the thumb. Being able to
read your thumbs helps potential employers to understand your concept
direction. Visuals should be quickly sketched or traced into position. Body
copy should be indicated with parallel lines. These lines represent the
placement and the amount of room the copy might take up when written.

You will rarely have a thumb that ends up as your final design choice.
It is more likely that two or more will be combined to create the overall
look of the final ad. The point is to have multiple options in front of you.
This allows you to change your mind or introduce new ideas into the
design mix.

Thumbnails allow you to work anywhere; it is difficult even for professional designers to be creative on demand a few hours before a dead-

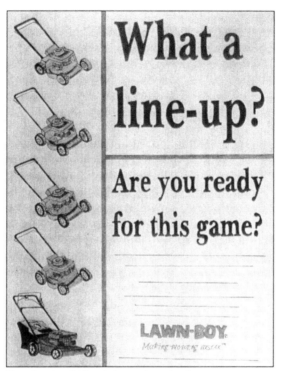

Roughs should be tight to show both concept
development and design skills.

line. Think about what you need to accomplish, and let it fester a few
hours or even a few days if time allows.

Being able to work fast is critical in design. Thought development and
then quick thumbnail sketches wipe out the pressure and anxiety associated with a blank page. Get any idea down; thinking ahead makes the
creative process a bit easier.

Roughs

Roughs or **layouts** are the third stage in the design process, and they are
chosen from your best thumbnail ideas. Professionals usually use roughs
as their idea-generation stage. Roughs are often presented to the client,
especially an established client. Roughs are done full size, or the size of
the final piece, and in color if relevant. Clients will usually see from three
to five design options at this stage.

If you are presenting concepts to a new client who has no representative typeface or wishes to change their product/service image, offer alternative type choices on each rough. This allows them to see the typeface on the page, within the design and with any visuals or the logo. The image or personality each typeface projects for the company, service, or product plays an important visual role in the development of an identity or brand image. If a signature **type style** already exists for your client, continue to use that typeface on your roughs.

Each rough should include a different headline with a supporting subhead if required, as well as visual(s) and layout style if presenting multiple concepts. If you are creating a campaign series, each series should include at least three pieces and the concept should be evident in the headline, theme, character creation, repetitive layout style, and/or typeface.

Because clients, professors, peers, and eventually potential employers see roughs, the roughs should be tight, clean, and accurate. Use a ruler to draw the dimensions or frame of the ad as well as all body copy indication. Professional-looking layout and conceptual skills should shine here. Final ads will be reproduced on the computer.

All type—such as headlines, subheads, and slogans—should be accurately reproduced in position on the rough and in the representative typeface and weight. If you don't feel comfortable with drawing the type, set it first on the computer and then trace it into position on the rough. Body copy is still represented by using lines to show placement, width, height, and depth.

Don't worry if your hand skills or illustration skills are slightly less than perfect; a few drawing classes can tighten up those skills. Art directors are more conceptual designers than they are illustrators. A potential employer can overlook a whole lot of drawing sins if your conceptual skills are strong.

Visuals on a rough must be tight enough for the client to understand what is going on or what is being shown. Again, if your hand skills still need a little work, find one or more references, enlarge or reduce them as needed, and trace them into position.

The client will view all ideas. One may be chosen for publication; most likely, it will be sent back to creative for minor tweaks—or worse, a major overhaul.

Super Comprehensives

The final or fourth stage in the design process is known as **super comprehensives** or **super comps.** Although not technically a part of the design process, super comps are created from your final roughs. They are generated on the computer with all headlines, subheads, photographs and/or illustrations, a logo, and—for the first time—completed body copy in place, simulating exactly how the finished design will look and read. If body copy has not yet been completed, greeking may be used. **Greeking** is a haphazard arrangement of letters, numbers, punctuation, and paragraph breaks that is used to temporarily represent copy. This allows the client to see how text will look on the page.

The super comp is also an integral part of your portfolio and shows off additional and necessary talents. Not only do you get to flesh out your concept in your body copy, but you can showcase your layout and conceptual skills as well as your knowledge of the computer/software and production skills.

Ideally, the super comp will mimic the rough as closely as possible; however, this is your final opportunity to make any final adjustments to the design.

Every art director you interview with will be looking for something specific or unique to fill a need within their agency or department, so the best thing you can do is to be prepared. Hand skills, conceptual skills, and computer skills will not only address any and all *issues* or *needs* you will run into but also will make outshining the competition easier.

GEOMETRIC LAYOUTS

Being able to draw is often seen as critical to an art director's arsenal of talents. Although drawing skills are important, most designers will tell you the computer has all but eliminated that requirement and that the ability to come up with great ideas is far more important.

In the section on layout stages, we discussed how to set and trace type as well as how to size and trace visuals. This process, however, is very time consuming. Working with geometric shapes and/or organic shapes to create images can be a lot faster.

For nondesigners, the fastest way to lay out a page is to think of it in terms of geometric shapes. Headlines can be blocked out using various-sized rectangles in varying lengths, placing them in varying positions on the page.

Subheads can be represented as a series of zigzag lines. These lines can be of varying length and depth, and their placement should be considered (i.e., centered, flush left, flush right, justified). Boxes and lines should be clean and straight, creating structure.

If you're outlining or clarifying concept direction, it is recommended that you write out your headline and subhead as opposed to using geometric shapes. Showing is far superior to giving an explanation.

Visuals, whether shown alone or grouped, can be any shape, but those

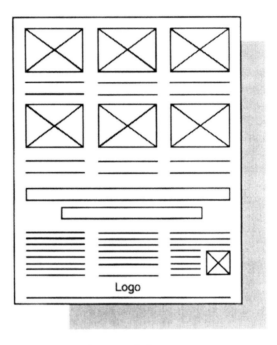

An example of geometric layout.

confined to boxes are usually rectangular or square. The box should have an X that runs from corner to corner, representing a visual.

Body copy, or the descriptive copy within an ad, is represented by placing parallel lines on the page to simulate body copy. Body copy position can vary from one to two or three columns. Lines should indicate whether copy will be centered, flush left, or justified. Consider creating faux paragraphs by indenting the first line about one-fourth inch and making the last line in the paragraph shorter than previous lines. This technique increases the visibility of white space on the page. Continue this technique for successive paragraphs. If you're using multiple columns of copy in your design, they should be of equal width and depth for balance.

The right column can be shorter than the left in order to place a visual or the logo in the copy, creating what is known as a *wrap.* Be sure to leave white space around wraps to increase readability. Width and depth must be constant and equal either way. Geometric and organic shapes can also be used to create abstract objects or visuals.

Remember the section on design principles? It pointed out the need to "have a purpose" to your layout choices by creating structure and harmony and avoiding confusion. Using an imaginary margin line that goes

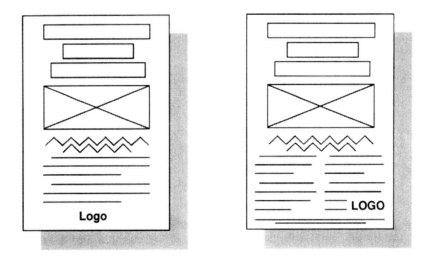

Geometric layouts. One column of copy with the logo centered at the bottom *(left)* and two columns of copy with a logo wrap balancing the right and left columns *(right).*

down the left side, or even a centerline, will help you with creating structure.

Every object imaginable can be broken down to simple geometric shapes and still be recognizable. When you're generating a thumbnail idea, this technique is much faster than finding a visual to trace. Working with basic shapes takes the fear out of layout, allowing for more time to work on design solutions.

For the nondesigner, using geometric and organic shapes to get your idea across is a viable alternative to detailed designs. Those looking for a design job need to highlight concept and basic layout skills.

The Page: Problems and Solutions

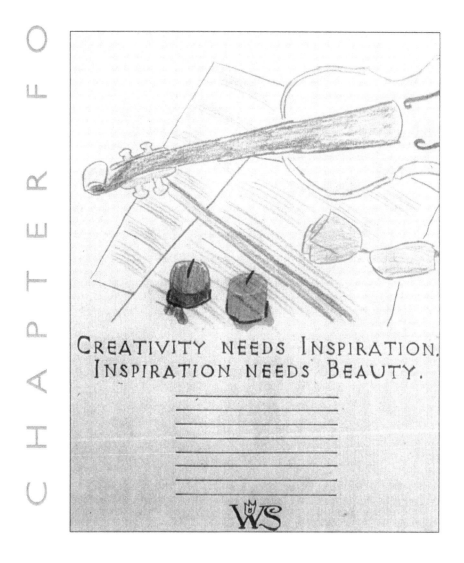

CHAPTER FOUR

CREATIVITY NEEDS INSPIRATION.
INSPIRATION NEEDS BEAUTY.

WHITE SPACE

Every well-designed ad should have white space. Basically this refers to the white of the paper, which is used in setting off and organizing elements contained in the ad as well as in bringing order to chaos. White space frames your ad and creates an elegant, sophisticated look. The less white space an ad has, the more cluttered or disjointed it appears. The amount of white space you use will depend on the design and the overall look you are trying to achieve.

Effective use of white space is the key to an organized design that enhances readability and legibility. **Readability** is achieved when a viewer can read an ad at a glance. **Legibility** refers to whether, in that short look, they understood the message.

The strategic use of white space is your first line of defense in the battle for readership. White space creates a stopping place for the eye, making reading easier. White space also brings order to a page. By design-

An example of a good use of white space.

ing the page not only with layout techniques but also with white space, you can make an ad look organized—even an ad with too much to say and too many products.

Placing as much white space as possible around an object allows the eye to isolate one item at a time. Young designers often want to fill every inch of space within an ad. Remember that structure, balance, and eye flow—as well as a dose of white space—are the keys to good design.

Eye flow is critical to understanding an ad's message. As readers, we are trained from day one to read from the top of the page to the bottom; and from left to right. Altering this simple pattern by placing unrelated photos or floating text within an ad creates confusion, causing consumers to miss important points or visuals. No one will work at reading an ad. If the consumer is confused or frustrated, she'll just turn the page.

The lack of white space in an ad can indicate the quality of the store and the products it sells. In the consumer's mind, clutter means low budget. On the other hand, the more white space there is, the more elegant the ad becomes; the design is thus creating the illusion of expense. It's not always about what you say, but how the viewer perceives it.

Unfortunately, you will have very little control over how many items your client wishes to place in an ad. You do have control over placement. Group things when you can, or separate them by confining them in a grid pattern.

Always consider white space when determining the inside margins of an ad. **Margins** are the white space that appears between the inside edges of an ad and where the copy or visual elements begin. Margins can be almost any size, but they should be no less than one-fourth inch on all four sides. An ad with the white of the page as a design element may have as much as two or three inches of white space surrounding the text or visuals. Text that wraps around visuals should create a relationship, not a feud. Text and visuals should look cozy, but not indifferent; one is being used to explain the other. There should be at least one-fourth inch of space between columns of text or between text and visuals. These are starting points; there are no definitive laws. Consistency is key to a strongly structured design.

THE WHITE-HOLE PHENOMENON

When you're using large amounts of white space, be sure to use it around text and visuals and not haphazardly between or beside them. Apply white space uniformly. Do not let the reader fall into a white hole. White holes are created when headlines or visuals are too small, when there is not enough body copy, or when the designer has pushed a headline or logo

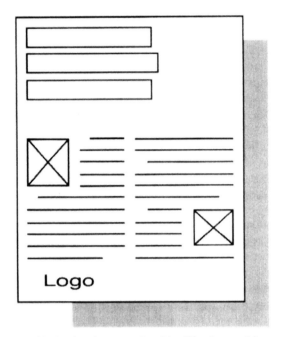

Avoid shoving items to the side. Distribute white
space evenly to avoid creating holes or dead
space.

too far to one side. The result is a white hole, or useless space. The client
pays for a complete message, not a partial one. Have a point—a reason for
your design choices. Never shove type to one side or stagger it unless you
have a visual to fill the resulting hole(s) or are repeating the pattern elsewhere in the ad.

A white hole signals that something is wrong with the design. Consider breaking text into additional lines, enlarging it, or both. Holes can
also be created when ads are not in balance, such as when logos are left to
float aimlessly at the bottom right of an ad. The resulting hole on the left
could have been filled simply by adding more text to the left column,
balancing it with the logo in the right column, or by centering the logo at
the bottom of the page. Additional options include enlarging visuals or
adding a visual or two to the copy.

DOMINANT ELEMENTS

Every ad needs to have a dominant element, one thing that really draws
the viewer's eye. This element can be the headline, a visual, or a grouping

There should
have been an
Oreo cookie
in this ad,
but someone
in creative
was hungry.

Oreo, They're for everyone.

OREO

This dominant type example has something
important to say. Don't be afraid to scream the
message.

of visuals. Not everything in an ad is of equal importance, even though
the client may think so. Only one thing can best advance your concept,
unique selling proposition (USP), or big idea, and it should be obvious.

Type That Has Something to Say

After the logo, the most important piece of text on the page is the **headline.**
For it to dominate, the headline must be large, very bold, or both. It should
send a message and be able to stand on its own. Taking left- and right-
brain characteristics into consideration, use headline text as the dominant
design element when you have something important to say.

Visuals That Have Something to Show

Visuals tell the story in pictures. A dominant visual can free up the whole
page. Visual options include featuring the product with or without a back-

There is more than one way to show a story. The product alone (*left*), the product placed in a setting (*middle*), and the product in use (*right*).

ground, in use, placed in a setting, or all alone on the page. A dominant visual can be created by taking multiple related visuals and grouping them, thus creating a presence with weight. Use visuals as the dominant design element when you have something important to show your viewers.

Using the Dominant Element

Whichever option you choose—headlines or visuals—the dominant design element must have a point. It should work to further promote the visual/verbal message.

So which works best? Although there are no set rules, dominant headlines have greater presence on a newspaper page, whereas visuals have greater presence on a magazine page. Since a newspaper page is overwhelmingly gray, especially when viewed peripherally, a large block of black draws attention. A large amount of white space appears to the eye at first as a hole, drawing attention in a different way. Reproduction problems encountered in newspaper make photos look flat; they recede into the

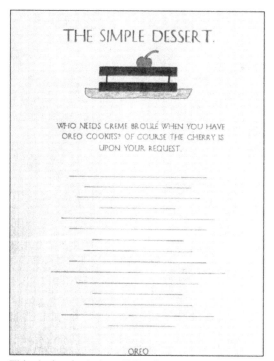

This design includes all five layout elements.

page. Just the opposite is true in magazine advertising. Strong blacks and whites are the ticket to attention-getting newspaper ads, and the strategic use of color sets a tone or creates an image in magazine.

COMPONENTS THAT MAKE UP AN AD: WHAT GOES WHERE?

There is no right or wrong answer to the question of what goes where in an ad, but there are some solid rules of thumb to consider. An ad can be nothing more than a visual, or it can be extremely copy heavy. As long as it's informative, advances the product's image, and creates interest in the minds of consumers, you're on the right track. But as young designers, you'll want to set up a few absolutes and some safety nets.

Any ad can be made up of the following five elements, in varied order: headline, subhead(s), visual(s), body copy, and logo. Not every component

This design includes four out of five layout elements. The headline says it all—eliminating the need for a subhead.

needs to be present in every ad; however, order is somewhat predetermined, especially for young designers. You want to show potential employers that you know how to use all five components, and that you know when—and when not—to use them.

The order in which components appear depends on the concept being emphasized. If the headline has a great consumer benefit or is extremely important to the ad's direction, then it goes first; place it at the top of the design. If the visual says more than words can, then place it at the top of the design. This thought process also will help you to determine which component, copy, or visual should be the dominant component on the page.

Consider trying some of the following layout options (read each column separately, top to bottom, for order of design elements):

Head	Head	Visual	Head
Subhead	Visual	Headline	Visual
Visual	Subhead	Subhead	Subhead
Body Copy	Body Copy	Body Copy	Visual
Logo	Logo	Logo	Body Copy + Visual
			Logo

These are certainly not the only layout options available to a designer, but they should be considered a good place to start. Each option allows the designer to feature either the headline or the visual.

TALKING TO YOUR TARGET

As ad designers, when we target a consumer group, we look at specific characteristics and lifestyle conditions. We may target a group of similar individuals, but we do not talk to all of them in our advertising. When writing body copy or developing a headline or visual, we must target and speak to only one individual within that target. This approach allows the reader to create a connection between the product and their own lives. By creating strong visual/verbal relationships, we can talk to the target like an old friend.

Headlines That Steal the Show

A headline must always be the first piece of copy, whether it appears above or below a visual. The headline is either shouting your concept direction or

Magazine. Note how the type does not overwhelm the
photograph.

supporting it. A headline can be a statement (phrase) or it can be one or
more complete sentences. Headlines are of indeterminate length, but usually
range from one- to seven-word statements to one to two sentences in length.
Newspaper advertising requires an ad that draws attention, so a statement in
large type often works best. Headlines used in a magazine should have
dignity, a sense of blending with the other elements on the page.

A headline's job is to stand out in the crowd, to be noticed and unfor-
gettable. Good headlines often announce a consumer benefit to entice the
consumer into the ad; but they can also pose a question, give an instruc-
tion, or entice the reader through misdirection.

Including a consumer benefit helps inform your target how the product
can benefit them in their daily life. Good research efforts make identifying
a consumer benefit more individualistic. When the ad offers a highly targeted benefit, the consumer can view himself using the product.

Headlines should have a presence on the page, not only because of
what they say but also because of how they look and sound. Headlines

Newspaper. The bold type used in this ad
screams off of the page.

should not be blocky, nor should they be pushed too far to one side of the ad. Enlarge a headline that is too small, or break it differently to equalize space.

If your headline currently breaks into three lines, consider breaking it into four lines and enlarging it. Every headline should have a "sense of rhythm associated with the line breaks," says Roy Paul Nelson in his book *The Design of Advertising*. Nelson goes on to explain that "a headline should sound as though the copywriter tapped their foot while writing it." This is a great analogy for hearing the sound associated with line breaks. But be careful where you break; avoid slicing up proper nouns, and rewrite if necessary.

Once the rhythm is set, it's time to look at the breaks. Consider breaking large text—like headlines and subheads—into short, long, short, long

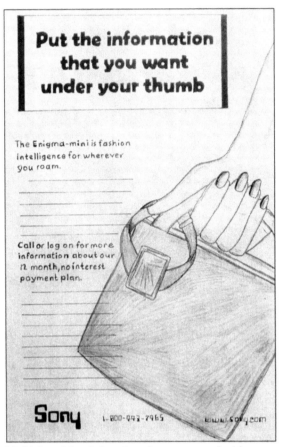

Multiple subheads break up long copy and add strong
blacks to the page.

lines or long, short, long, short lines. This helps to create white space and
keeps the type from looking blocky.

If your headline does its job, readers should continue through the ad
to the body copy, or descriptive copy. This is where the sale is finalized.
If your headline does not provoke reader interest, they will never read the
body copy and envision the product or service in their lives. If your headline can communicate both visually and verbally, you may not even need
body copy. "Tear. Wipe. Done. Cleaning Is So Labor Intensive." It
doesn't get more visual/verbal than that.

A headline needs to seduce. An advertised sales message is not a chosen read; it's what I refer to as an enticed read. The target consumers are
enticed into the informative or benefit-related headline through only a brief

glance. If their interest has been sparked, we've got them, and they opt to read on.

A Subhead's Response

Immediately following the headline, the next piece of copy should be a **subhead,** if you are using one. A subhead's job is to explain in more detail what the headline is saying, to elaborate on the statement or comment made, or to answer the question posed. Ideally, the subhead should not be another statement, but one or two complete sentences. Each subhead relates to the content of the copy below it.

A visual should be the only element that appears between the headline and subhead. These two design elements work together to whet the consumer's appetite, compelling him to read the body copy.

The subhead is the second largest piece of copy on the page. The headline and subhead should be set in the same **typeface** and **type style,** although they can be of different weights. Multiple subheads can be used throughout lengthy body copy to give the eye a rest and break up the page into more pleasing blacks and whites. Additional subheads should read like chapter headings and need not be complete sentences. A consumer should be able to quickly glance through the subheads and know where the copy is going.

The aliens from Mars brought green clowns to chase the local anteater. Bundles and bundles of blankets cover the apple tree to prevent gravity. Ten cars recently jumped over the moon and landed on some day old cheese.

The polka dot cat rode to work in his blue mouse car, before being pulled over for bad taste. The local lumber jack wears red long johns rather than blue overalls. Uncle Bucky waits at the bank to take your money. The big brass band changed into new uniforms.

The big yellow chicken sat on her head and crowed while the old woman stuck her tongue out at the passing wild flowers.

The great blues man played his saxophone late into the night lulling the neighbors to sleep, by dreaming about buses and cotten candy.

The brown spotted wiener dog chased the yellow spotted cat to school and then bit a whisker.

The dog jumped through the hoop

This example shows a widow at the top and an orphan at the bottom of the second column.

Body Copy That Informs

The **body copy** is the nuts and bolts, the heart and soul of your ad. Newspaper copy should describe the product in detail, highlighting specific features like price, size, color, materials used in the product's construction, and so forth. Magazine copy should build an image for your product or service.

Readability and legibility are critical here; this is where the sale or inquiry is made. Body copy is not quite the smallest copy in an ad. It is often set in a different typeface from that of the headline and subhead, usually due to readability at a smaller size. It is recommended to keep the same type style, that is, serif or sans serif, throughout a design. This is not an absolute rule, but consistency of style is required to unify the design.

Copy dealing with addresses, phone numbers, Web addresses, credit card information, e-mail addresses, store hours, parking, and so on is referred to as **detail copy.** It should be in the same face as the body copy and no smaller than eight or nine points for readability purposes.

Body copy can be set up in multiple columns, or as a single body of type. It is easiest to read when set flush to the left or justified. Long lines of text are difficult to read, so limit single blocks of copy to a maximum of six inches in width. If you have a lot of copy, consider breaking it into two or even three separate columns if space allows. As a general rule, copy columns are anywhere from three to four inches wide.

Look out for widows or orphans. A **widow** is a single word or a short line that appears at the top of a page or at the top of a new column of copy. An **orphan** is a short line that appears at the bottom of a page, or a word (or part of a word) on a line by itself at the end of a paragraph. The first line in a paragraph should never end up at the bottom of the page or column all alone. If at least two lines will not fit, move the line to the next column or page. Text may need to be rewritten or enlarged to correct the problem.

Detail copy usually appears near the bottom of the ad, near the logo. As designers, we want the consumer to see the store name and learn all she needs to know about visiting the store in one place. The detail copy can appear above or below the logo, often on a single line with bullets or small dots separating copy points. If you are using a map in your ad, the detail information might be stacked in a column either under or alongside of the logo. Remember, if you're using these last few options, to be sure the bottom of the ad is balanced.

VISUAL OPTIONS

A visual can be a photograph, an illustration, line art, or graphic design. Its main function is to show the product in detail, and often while in use.

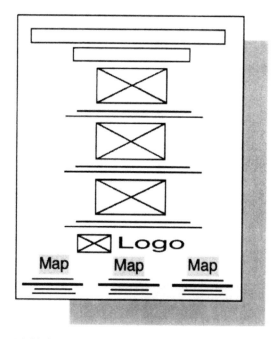

Multiple maps are used to balance the bottom of this ad.

The visuals should relate to what is being said or alluded to in the headline, creating a visual/verbal relationship—or, more simply put, each of your visuals needs to have a point. Visuals can be placed almost anywhere within an ad. They can appear between the headline and the subhead, between the subhead and the body copy, and even in the body copy itself.

Logos and Slogans

The **logo** is a company or product's symbol. It should be prominently displayed at either the bottom right or the bottom center of an ad. A logo can consist of nothing more than the company or product name, represented typographically; it can also be a graphic symbol, or a combination of type and graphic. A logo needs to close every ad, even if it's used in the headline. It needs to be the last thing the viewer sees.

The **slogan** represents the company's philosophy or a product's image. It is usually placed either above or below the logo. The two are a unit and should always be used together. A slogan is usually a three- to seven-word phrase.

Do I Need a Map?

Maps are ugly, and they take up valuable design space. But if you live in a large city, they are indispensable. Be sure to show major highways and intersections. Driving directions may be included and should point out landmarks. Avoid references to north and south; instead, directions should specify location in terms of left and right.

Sometimes several maps are needed to show multiple store locations. Consider grouping them at the bottom of the ad, creating a section devoted to directions. Place the logo alongside, above, or below the map section.

Announcement Devices

Important sale information can be highlighted through announcement devices such as snipes, bursts, or banners. A **burst** looks like a fireworks

These ads contain banners used as graphic devices.

Simplify

Make your own simple, additive-free peanut butter.

The Peanut Buster for only $52.95

RICH'S

Monday - Saturday 10 am to 9 pm,   1866 Peachtree Avenue
Sunday Noon to 6 pm.   555-555-6046

DISCOVER   VISA

If you have something important to say, placing it in a
banner helps the message pop off of the cluttered page.

explosion; a **snipe** is a black triangular shape, usually placed in a top corner of the ad. Black bars, or **banners,** ideally are placed at the top of
an ad. These bars can also be used as page dividers, making important
announcements stand out. The type appearing in these black blocks reverses to white or a light color, and should be set in a larger, bolder typeface—usually 18- to 24-point type—to ensure readability and legibility.
Announcement devices like bursts and snipes should not be considered for
the more elegant or pricey sales; they can have an outcast or desperate
feel, as if there is no permanent place for them elsewhere.

An example of big type.

LAYOUT STYLES

An ad's personality can be expressed through the layout style, or how its components are featured within the design.

What does your concept say about itself? Will you be using lots of white space, for an elegant feel? Will you insert a dominant photograph to draw the viewer's attention? Are you incorporating multiple small illustrations, scattered throughout the copy, to instruct the viewer how to use the product or service? Do you want to section off the ad, to show the viewer multiple benefits?

Think of layout styles as the clothes for your concept. Does it shout sporty, sophisticated, or modern? Does it demand attention through words, or is a visual worth a thousand words? When you're designing, it's doubly important to consider what you want the ad to project visually to the consumer, as well as what it says. Let's look at nine of the most commonly used layout styles.

Big type	Multipanel
Circus	Picture window
Copy heavy	Rebus
Frame	Silhouette
Mondrian	

Big Type

The *big-type* layout style is used when the headline is the focal point within the ad. If your product or service can boast a definitive consumer benefit, then the ad should shout that benefit from the rooftop in very large type. Visuals play a secondary role here. The ad's beauty and appeal are defined by the typeface and what it says. Size and weight of type will often vary, but should project a distinct pattern. The static appearance of this layout style is actually very clean and concise. Type works as a graphic, creating mood. If pictures are included, they are small and do not compete with what is being said. If you love the shape, texture, and movement of type, the opportunities to use it as a graphic, verbal element are wide open in this layout style.

Circus

The *circus* layout style uses everything from the designer's arsenal within the ad. It is not unusual to see multiple type sizes and faces, with assorted snipes and bursts touting grand openings and sale dates in brazenly reversed text. In this layout, there are always too many unrelated visuals to even think about grouping them in an organized fashion. These ads scream chaos. The key is controlling that chaos. Consider using a grid layout, combining or grouping components to focus on one dominant image. Try to create as much white space as is humanly possible. This attempt at structure aids in manipulating the viewer's eye movement in a more controlled fashion, allowing them to move from component to component or

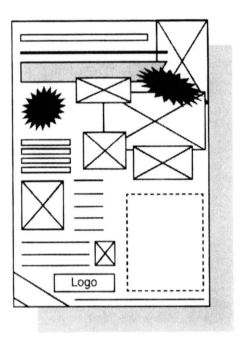

Circus layout. This ad features multiple
bursts—very busy, very scary. This type of
layout should be avoided at all costs.

from geometric block to geometric block without missing anything. Structure also alleviates that floating look and grounds the design, giving it
more power.

Copy Heavy

Headlines and visuals take a backseat in the *copy-heavy* layout style. Instead, the focus is on the body copy. A large amount of body copy is used
to introduce a product or service. Visuals, if present, are small and are
used to show the product or logo. Copy-heavy layouts are a great choice
for young creatives wishing to promote their copywriting skills.

Frame

Frame layouts are most often featured in newspaper advertising, when it's
important to isolate your ad from surrounding text. Frames or borders can

A copy heavy example.

be of any weight or design, and they often define ad size. Frames can be simple unobtrusive lines, pin-striped, detailed, created via colored backgrounds, or illustrative in nature.

Mondrian

If you're familiar with the works of Dutch painter Piet Mondrian, you'll understand why the *Mondrian* layout style screams sections. Here, multiple geometric blocks of text, graphic shapes, color, and/or shaded areas are used to separate parts of the ad and guide the reader through the copy. Each geometrically or organically shaped section focuses on an element within the ad, such as headlines, body copy, and varied uses for the product. This layout style uses bold shapes and color to make it stand out among the clutter of other ads or editorial material. By isolating single elements, the designer ensures that each element is viewed independently.

This simple frame border with graphic
accents draws the eye into the visual.

Mondrian example.

Solid geometric shapes such as circles, squares, rectangles, triangles, and lines are used to further isolate specific sections; but they give the ad an almost three-dimensional feel when it's strategically placed near large areas of white space. By placing bright colors within selected shapes, or reversing text out of a colored background, you can draw the reader's eye—so show or say something important here. You have them; take advantage.

Multipanel

The *multipanel* layout style uses pictures with captions to tell a story, or to feature multiple products set up in equal-sized boxes. These boxes are placed side by side, either butted up against each other or separated by a small amount of white space. Smaller inset photographs can be placed over one large photograph to point out details. Body copy is often replaced with copy captions, located either within the panel or under each picture.

Multipanel example.

This layout style works very well when showing is more important then telling, when comparing one product to another, or when bringing a television storyboard to print.

Picture Window

The *picture-window* layout style features one large photograph, often with the headline overprinting the photograph. Type can be a solid color, or it can be reversed out of the background. This layout style is best used when you want the reader to participate in the photo. Example, your photo might picture a small sailboat and a beautiful sunset. The headline might read, "Wish You Were Here?"

When you're placing type over a photograph, it is important to make sure the type can be read easily. Type should be placed over a quiet portion of the photo, that is, the lightest part of the sunset, not the active portion—the sailboat, trees, and so forth. Also be sure that the typeface is readable

Picture window example.

against the background. A sunset has a lot of color changes, so you may have to enlarge the type or choose a bolder typeface or weight. The key to this layout style is creating a close relationship between text and visual.

Rebus

The layout style known as the *rebus* is usually crammed full with visuals. Working in tandem with the body copy, visuals are often placed within the text to help illustrate the story. Pictures can also be used as substitutes for words within headlines. This is an elegant layout style that lends itself well

Rebus example.

to instructional copy, where a picture can be used to demonstrate copy points. Text can be wrapped around an image, visually isolating its content to what is being shown. Visuals can be repetitive in size or alternate from small to large in order to create focal points.

Silhouette

The *silhouette* layout style relies on the grouping of visual elements within an ad. The group of items becomes the dominant element within the ad. A large amount of white space usually surrounds the grouped items, setting them off even more. This layout style works great when you have multiple products to be featured within an ad. All too often when working with multiple elements, young designers set them up in what I call the "friend-less" arrangement. Each element is set apart from the others, often in a straight line, to be left floating all alone on the page. By grouping elements in pleasing and even irregular shapes, you can give weight to the visuals and create eye flow.

This silhouette example features callouts.

Placing prices in the headline makes a bold
statement.

If you have type that must accompany each element, consider using
callouts. **Callouts** are small amounts of copy appearing alongside or below
an individual image and connected by a small line. Text is descriptive and
might feature price points. Be sure to balance the callouts evenly around
the visual. This layout style works well when the visual breaks up the
headline or the copy, or when type is slightly overlaid on a visual, or vice
versa. White space is at a premium when items are grouped. At times
the silhouette layout style can just be too static; to alter its symmetrical
appearance, consider allowing items to touch the edges of the ad in oppos-
ing spots.

So Which Layout Style Should I Use, and What's Important?

There are no right or wrong rules as to which layout style(s) are best suited
to a specific media. The only guidelines are those regarding product image
and readability and legibility issues.

Look first to your concept, and then consider how that message will be delivered and perceived. Readability and legibility issues—along with those concerning print quality, structure, and balance—will play a key role in your choice of layout style, typeface, or visual. Many components appearing in the ad are of equal importance; it's the designer's job to organize those elements into a cohesive package.

Components might include a screaming headline, sale dates, grand openings, new locations, and multiple products—each needing descriptive copy and/or price points. Usually several photographs or illustrations are needed to show the product(s). You may also need to add detail copy and a logo that will not get lost along the way. Each additional component will help you determine which layout style to use.

Organizing components is the key to success in any medium. Remember, even though an ad is cluttered, that one dominant image must prevail. Your job is to decide what that one dominant element should be. A large headline assists in announcing an event; placing a consumer benefit in the headline personalizes the sale; showing the product allows the consumer to interact with the product. Additional products can be smaller and placed lower in the ad in a grid or as a part of the body copy.

When newspaper is your medium, consider using one large price point that is associated with the headline. We are all attracted by price. Magazine design encourages your visual(s) to take center stage and dominate the page, often showing the product alone or in use. A large photograph or illustration attracts the eye—as does a group of several items, causing a large mass of tones, lines, sizes, color, and black-and-white contrasts.

CHAPTER FIVE

Things to Know about Type

Type Designs and Identifiers

Type is designed using one of two distinct forms: serif or sans serif. **Serif** type has feet or delicate appendages that protrude from the edges of the letters, as in the type you're now reading. These appendages can appear at either the top or bottom of a letterform. **Sans serif** type has no appendages.

Type is categorized by its typeface. **Typeface** refers to type of a specific, uniform design; typefaces are often named after their designer. The typeface is part of a larger type family, which includes all the sizes and styles of that typeface. A typical computer type family contains four fonts in these type styles: roman, italic, bold, and bold/italic in all type sizes. On computers, the word *font* is used synonymously with *typeface,* though they are not the same. A **font** consists of a complete character set in one typeface and style; for example, all italic uppercase and lowercase letters, numbers, and punctuation.

Almost every typeface comes in varying weights. **Weight** represents the thickness or thinness of the typeface's body. These weights can range in scale from ultra light, light, book, medium, demi bold, bold, ultra bold, and ultra black, to name just a few.

The Language of Type

Different type designs reflect different images, moods, or even gender. It's important to choose a typeface that reflects the image of your product or service. Serif type, because of its delicate lines, has a more feminine appeal. Sans serif type boasts straight, unadorned lines that give it a more masculine appearance. This masculine/feminine appeal can sometimes be achieved using differing weights of the same typeface. For example, Helvetica, a sans serif typeface, comes in so many weights that Helvetica Light—a stately, tall, and thin typeface—bears little resemblance to the bulky, stout-looking Helvetica Ultra Bold. Serif typefaces such as Goudy—a round, elegant, yet squat typeface—can represent both masculine and feminine products. The best place to begin when determining which typeface and style to use is to match them to the product's personality or the tone of the ad, and experiment from there.

Serif   Sans serif

Rockwell
Rockwell
Rockwell
Rockwell
Rockwell

(Top to bottom): Rockwell regular, italic, bold, bold italic, and extra bold

TYPE DESIGN RULES OF THUMB

When designing, the number of typefaces used in an ad should be controlled. The basic rule of thumb is two typefaces per design. The headline, subhead(s), announcement devices, and prices are usually set in the same typeface; the body copy and descriptive copy are set in another. There is no limit on the different weights that can be used within a design, but common sense should rule the day. Although there are no hard-and-fast rules about mixing serif and sans serif styles within an ad, it is best to use one style throughout the ad. The number of point sizes in an ad should also be controlled. An ad with multiple faces in various styles and sizes takes on a circus feel and is perceived as junky. However, any device, if used consistently and/or repetitively, avoids the need to play by the rules.

Logos are a graphic element and are not considered a typeface; they do not need to match the style of the advertised message.

Using type as a design element is becoming a lost art. Young designers do not realize, or do not wish to take the time to acquaint themselves with, the varying typefaces available to them beyond what comes on their computer.

This is where the computer is both sinner and saint. There are more typefaces available to you than what's on your computer—lots more. Designers before the computer age had hundreds of usable faces available to them. They were often manipulated before being used, creating a personalized look for a client's product or service, rather than the standard look of today's computer age.

TYPE SIZE AND CHARACTER

Type size is determined in points. **Points** are very small measurement devices; to help you out, there are 72 points to an inch. The height of a typeface's capital letters determines its point size. This can be misleading, since not all type faces are designed equally. Each typeface varies in weight and height, so not all 36-point uppercase letters will be the same height.

As you work—and become more familiar—with the various typefaces available to you, sizing will become less complicated.

Lowercase letters have two distinct features that are important to a designer—ascenders and descenders. **Ascenders** are the part of the letterform that extends upward and away from the body of a letter, as with the letters *b* and *d*. **Descenders** are the part of the letterform that projects downward below the **baseline,** or the imaginary line that type sits on, as with the letters *g* or *p*. Ascenders and descenders play a critical role in decisions concerning line spacing in design (known as leading in typography and in some computer programs) and a typeface's graphic appeal.

The amount of white space appearing between lines of copy can become a designer's trademark. If you like lines of text to be close together, with less white space appearing between lines, ascenders and descenders can often get in the way. This is where good old-fashioned type design or type manipulation comes into play. You might consider fusing an ascender from one line to a descender from another, or just chopping them off uniformly.

PUSHING TYPE AROUND: WHEN TO USE LINE SPACING OR LEADING

The terms *line spacing* and *leading* are both used to describe the amount of space between lines of text; however, they are job-class distinctive. The

bd gp

Ascenders *(left)* and
descenders *(right).*

Copy is funny any way you wink at it yet it allows you to ramble on no matter the date or time of day.

When the tiger reads he purrs with delight until the hyena nips him in the bud and attempts to steal his reading material. That would be okay but the tiger has a family to educate on top of everything else.

Kicky copy raises the hair on the back of the porcupines' neck. He prefers a good mystery about the Savanna any day of the week. The plots are much more interesting and he may have met one or two of the characters.

Termites love to read at breakfast, it tastes the same to them no matter the genre. Color offers an especially tasty treat, better than eating a cactus or carcass in the a.m. It's also a family affair to be shared on a warm summer night with the kids, grandma and the neighboring mounds.

12-point type with 12-point leading.

term **line spacing** is used when designing, and it refers to the amount of white space showing between lines of text. **Leading** (rhymes with "heading") is a term used in both printing and desktop publishing that gives a specific numerical value (measured in points) to the amount of white space appearing between lines of text.

For example, body copy could be 10 point, with 11 points of leading between lines of text. This means the line spacing, or white space between lines of text, will be slightly more than the height of a 10-point capital letter. Leading is measured from baseline to baseline of the type, and in this example it is the height or depth of an 11-point capital letter.

The amount of white space left between lines of text is a design choice. But there are some basic rules of thumb. Leading that is very tight, or uses less white space between lines, is usually used in larger text such as a headline or subhead. The leading would then be less than the point size of the type. How much less depends on how tight you like lines of text to be. Type that is set on itself (also referred to as *set solid*) would be used for smaller text, such as body copy. In this case, the leading is the same size as the type size. Body copy is easiest to read with at least one point of leading between lines of text, or 10-point type with 11-point lead-

Copy is funny any way you wink at it yet it allows you to ramble on no matter the date or time of day.

When the tiger reads he purrs with delight until the hyena nips him in the bud and attempts to steal his reading material. That would be okay but the tiger has a family to educate on top of everything else.

Kicky copy raises the hair on the back of the porcupines' neck. He prefers a good mystery about the Savanna any day of the week. The plots are much more interesting and he may have met one or two of the characters.

Termites love to read at breakfast, it tastes the same to them no matter the genre. Color offers an especially tasty treat, better than eating a cactus or carcass in the a.m. It's also a family affair to be shared on a warm summer night with the kids, grandma and the neighboring mounds.

12-point type with 14-point leading.

ing. You can go as small as 9-point type if space is a problem. Size will depend on the typeface chosen. Readability is enhanced if body copy is at least 10 on 10, 10 on 11, 11 on 11, or even 11 on 12. By increasing the amount of space between lines of text, the ad designer creates white space and makes reading smaller text easier.

SNUGGLE UP OR MOVE OVER: WHEN TO USE LETTERSPACING OR KERNING

Letterspacing, also known as **kerning,** is the removal or addition of white space between letterforms. *Kerning* is a term, used in both printing and desktop publishing, in which a numerical value (measured in points), most often a negative one, is given to the space between letters; *letterspacing* is a design term.

Copy is funny any way you wink at it yet it allows you to ramble on no matter the date or time of day.

When the tiger reads he purrs with delight until the hyena nips him in the bud and attempts to steal his reading material. That would be okay but the tiger has a family to educate on top of everything else.

Kicky copy raises the hair on the back of the porcupines' neck. He prefers a good mystery about the Savanna any day of the week. The plots are much more interesting and he may have met one or two of the characters.

Termites love to read at breakfast, it tastes the same to them no matter the genre. Color offers an especially tasty treat, better than eating a cactus or carcass in the a.m. It's also a family affair to be shared on a warm summer night with the kids, grandma and the neighboring mounds.

12-point type with 16-point leading.

Certain letter combinations appearing together can be problematic, for example, the capital letters RA. A word set in all caps, such as EN-TRANCE, has spacing problems. If you squint at the letterforms, you will see where there appears to be a hole between the RA and the AN as compared to the other letterforms. By kerning, or tightening up the space between these letters, the designer can alleviate holes that can make one word look like two. Kerning of individual letters should be a designer's secret. The viewer should not be able to detect kerning. Serif typefaces allow us to overlap serifs very comfortably when problem areas arise.

Tightening the letterspacing and line spacing allows you to enlarge your headline, creating a more elegant or dominant image that draws the consumer in. Because of their size, headlines need the most design/letterspacing attention, with subheads following close behind. Very little ma-

Copy is funny any way you wink at it yet it allows you to ramble on no matter the date or time of day.

When the tiger reads he purrs with delight until the hyena nips him in the bud and attempts to steal his reading material. That would be okay but the tiger has a family to educate on top of everything else.

Kicky copy raises the hair on the back of the porcupines' neck. He prefers a good mystery about the Savanna any day of the week. The plots are much more interesting and he may have met one or two of the characters.

Termites love to read at breakfast, it tastes the same to them no matter the genre. Color offers an especially tasty treat, better than eating a cactus or carcass in the a.m. It's also a family affair to be shared on a warm summer night with the kids, grandma and the neighboring mounds.

12-point type with 18-point leading.

nipulation is needed on body copy other than increasing the line spacing when space allows.

Eyeballing Type

Eyeballing refers to what type looks like after manual adjustments are made to line spacing or letterspacing. Each line of text should begin with

ENTRANCE
ENTRANCE

Large text often needs individual tweaking between letterforms. Do not be afraid to touch or overlap serifs.

equal leading. However, type is a visual animal and may need independent "tweaking" from line to line, depending on the letterforms appearing in the headline. After manipulation, the goal is to have all lines appear to have equal spacing, even though they may not. You do not want one line or combination of letters to appear tighter than the others. They must match visually, not mathematically. Visual adjustments are common when an unwanted descender from one line bumps into an ascender from the line below, or when certain letter combinations appear together.

TYPE ALIGNMENT

There are several ways that type can be laid out in an ad. The first is center on center, where type is set with one line centered above another. Alternating the length of line breaks can create more white space within the ad.

The next most common alignment is flush left, ragged right. This is where all lines of text begin in the same place—along the left margin of the ad. The right side of each line is of varying lengths. *Ragged* is the opposite of *flush*. You can also set type flush right, rag left. This alignment is most often used when working with two columns of type that wrap around a centrally placed visual.

The last type alignment option is justified. This is where each line of text begins in the same place along the left margin and ends in the same place at the right margin. This option is not used often in advertising design, because type has to be designed to fit within this type of format. Justified type often leaves large gaps between words, stretches out a long word, or creates multiple hyphens at the ends of lines. Justified type is great for newspaper articles; but it does not look good, nor is it easy to read, in advertising copy.

center on center

flush left, rag right

flush right, rag left

justified

flush left, rag right, paragraph indents

READABILITY, LEGIBILITY, AND DESIGN

One of the greatest challenges to advertisers is convincing people they need advertising. The fact is that very few people will admit to wanting to see advertising. So it's important to make sure, when readers are glancing at a newspaper or flipping through a magazine, that the advertiser's message is clear enough to be quickly read and understood. As designers, our goal is to get the reader to stop and spend time with an ad by reading it from start to finish.

It is important that all advertising be readable and legible at a glance. Be careful not to overdesign your type. Type that has been letterspaced or line spaced (kerned or leaded) too tightly becomes a blob, not a design element. Type that is too open becomes a white hole. Design your type where needed, and let the rest go.

Larger headlines can have tighter letterspacing and line spacing than smaller ones can, without affecting readability and legibility. Avoid, at all costs, using decorative typefaces such as scripts or anything with elaborate swishes or gothic appeal. Any time the reader has to slow down—or worse yet, reread—when looking at a headline, the ad creates apathy and triggers short attention spans, possibly causing the target to turn the page. No one wants to work at understanding an advertisement.

Type size directly affects readability. Catch the reader's eye with large text; whet their appetite with medium-sized text; sell the product with the smaller text; and tell them what they need to know about where and how to shop with the smallest text. If you're using any secondary subheads or banners, they should be slightly smaller than the main subhead. Your ad might look something like this.

Headline: 50 points
Leading of 48 points
Main subhead: 24 points, with
Leading of 22 points
Secondary subhead: 18 points, with
Leading of 16 points
Banner: 20 points
Body copy: 11 points, with
Leading of 12 points
Detail copy: 8 points, with
Leading of 9 points

TYPE FAUX PAS

Readability and legibility can be adversely affected by several design faux pas. Let's look at a few of the most common.

All Caps

Using all capital letters anywhere in an ad should be avoided. Consider it only when your headline is no more than one to three words long. Most people are not familiar with an all-caps format, and as a result they must read slower.

ABCDEFGHIJKLMN OPQRSTUVWXYZ

All caps.

Reverse Copy

Traditionally, type is set with black letters on a white background. Reverse text uses white or light-colored text on a black or dark-colored background. Again, using reversed text in large blocks of copy should be avoided. Readability is minimized because the format is unfamiliar. Reverse text works best for banner announcements, like those advertising grand openings or sale hours.

Reverse.

Italics

Italics should also be avoided, due to the same readability issues discussed earlier. Use italics sparingly; its best use is for emphasis, to set off a special word or phrase, a quotation, or a foreign word.

ABCDEFGHIJKLMN

OPQRSTUVWXYZ

All italicized caps.

Decorative Faces

Fancy or froufrou typefaces have no place in newspaper or magazine advertising. All their elaborate flourishes and decorative appearance make readability and legibility almost impossible at a glance.

Decorative faces.

TYPE AS A GRAPHIC ELEMENT

If you look at type, really look, you will see its beauty beyond content. Its form alone is a graphic device. Each face portrays a personality, an individualism that takes shape via content. The very randomness of the letterforms creates a uniform message with character and flair. Whether it's childish, traditional, expensive, or shabby chic, each typeface awaits the shape and expression given it by the designer.

Each typeface's personality should match the image projected by the product or service. However you decide to manipulate type—whether you alter the face by condensing or expanding it, or by increasing or decreasing the letter, word, or line spacing, type size, or line length—readability and legibility should take precedence over design.

Readability and legibility are also affected by the color and direction of type. A typeface does not have to be black. It can be any dark color such as brown, navy, forest green, or maroon, to name a few. Light- or pastel-colored faces lack contrast against the stark white of the printed page, making them difficult to see and again slowing readers down, making them reread in order to understand the message.

Type does not have to be set horizontally. Alternatives include running headlines or announcements vertically down the side of the page. This is a great idea if you are considering designing in an asymmetrical format. Type set on an angle or on a curve should be used sparingly. Not only is readability affected, but the overall look of your design suffers, creating a cluttered, unruly look. If you must set type on a curve or angle, repeat the pattern somewhere else in the ad or run it around a visual, matching the shapes.

CHAPTER SIX

Newspaper: What's the Big Design Deal?

WHAT IS NEWSPAPER ADVERTISING?

Newspaper advertising, also known as **retail advertising,** must accomplish two things. The first is to sell a product or service, and the second is to entice the reader into a response. This is a tough job. The reader has to digest an enormous amount of written information before noticing your client or company's ad amid the maze of an indistinguishable gray page that characteristically makes up an average newspaper page.

Newspaper engages the reader by using bold headlines, juicy got-to-have-it sales, new and improved claims, and coupons. No matter what claim or approach you're using, your job as a designer or account executive is to figure out how to make your client's ad stand out.

Put yourself in the consumer's place. What catches your eye, and what do you need to know? How do I use it? Where can I find it? Why can't I live without it? The answers can be found through meticulous message construction and the use of a few simple layout techniques.

Designing for newspaper isn't difficult, but it is strategic, and a good design plan needs specific tactics. Be sure you have a strong concept and a headline that informs or includes a consumer benefit. You must feature your product and promote its price. Each layout should create strong black-and-white contrasts, feature one dominant element, promote price or availability, and use white space effectively. Type should be easy to read and be brand or image specific. The ad should flow easily from element to element, closing with the logo and detail copy to make shopping easier.

Visuals can be cropped in many ways. Show only what is necessary and delete the rest. *Assignment courtesy of* Visual Literacy.

The simple, inexpensive, yet informative nature of newspaper advertising makes it one of the leading advertising vehicles.

Advertising appearing in newspaper falls into two distinct categories: local (including classified and display) and national.

Local Retail Advertising

The term *local advertising* has two meanings: the first is that the advertising is of a local nature and tells readers where in their area they can find the product. The second meaning is that the advertising was initiated locally.

The Worth of the Paper It's Printed On

The paper your ad is printed on directly affects the readability and legibility of type and the fine details within visuals. Newspapers are printed on a low-grade paper known as newsprint. Newsprint is classified as an uncoated paper stock, and it has a very high bleed or spread rate. Uncoated paper stocks are less expensive because they have not been treated to alleviate bleeding, so using newsprint lowers the cost of printing the newspaper.

Classified Advertising

Classified advertising is done in-house by local newspapers, and it deals with consumer buying and selling. Categories feature garage sales, auctions, job opportunities, and real estate opportunities, to name just a few.

Display Ads

Display ads can be either local or national. The name refers to the complete list of components appearing within an ad such as any visuals, type, or logos.

National or Brand-Name Advertising

National advertising features brand-name products that can be found at local establishments or acquired through toll-free phone numbers or Internet access. Carried in newspapers throughout the country, national advertising requires few modifications from city to city outside of personalizing maps and/or addresses.

VISUALS, OPTIONS, AND DECISIONS

The visual you choose to place in your ad design is important. It should take into consideration the media to be used as well as the product or service to be advertised. The visual your targets eventually see is a representation of the client's product or service. As the designer, you can decide how to present that image—perhaps through the reality of photography, or with the artistic expression of an illustration. You can achieve a more simplistic approach with black-and-white line art; or maybe the budget constraints call for clip or stock art. Whatever image becomes the visual voice of your client's product, be sure it supports your headline and concept, reflects the product's image, and can hold detail during printing.

Photographs

Photographs, especially those with people in them, can create a mood or conjure up emotions. Although photographs are expensive, consumers prefer them in ads promoting services such as banking, investing, or food products that are not prepackaged. Photographs can more easily show the product being used, and they allow consumers to envision themselves using the product or service.

Photographs give credibility to your product, and so do the models you choose for them. Don't use anyone who appears unlikely to use the product or service. Be sure they are suitably dressed as well as the right age and sex.

Large photographs reproduce best on newsprint. Do not use smaller photos when minute details need to be preserved.

Cropping

Cropping is the removal of any unnecessary part(s) of a photograph, allowing the designer to dispose of information that is not necessary to the design. For a viewer to understand what is going on or being shown in a photograph, it's often enough to include just part of an image and very little of its background. By using only what you need in a photograph to impart the ad's message, you can zoom in on emotions or important details.

Cropped images are usually placed inside boxes or next to an ad's border. This placement grounds an image, anchoring partial images or body parts so they don't seem to be floating on the page. Confining cropped photos to borders or at the edge of the page, such as with a **bleed** photograph, gives the illusion they are just entering our view or there is more to know.

Black-and-White Line Art

Black-and-white line art consists of a line drawing having no tonal qualities. A line drawing is a great choice when your ad is spotlighting products with small details, such as lace tablecloths or delicate china patterns. Drawings simplify a design and create a strong black-and-white contrast on the page, as opposed to photographs, which can cause the ad to recede on the page by graying down the design. Products presented as line art can be grouped, yet retain their individuality through the strategic use of contrast, shadows, highlights and details, volume, and varying textures. A strong black-and-white drawing retains details without muting quality.

But again, that darned old newsprint can be a problem. Your illustrators must know where, and how, the drawings are going to be used. Like some typefaces, line art has delicate details; if they get too fine, they can disappear during printing. Lines should be of medium to bold weights.

Illustrations

Illustrations have the same design and printing guidelines as those for photographs. Unlike line art, illustrations have tonal qualities; so they are more like a photograph. But unlike photographs, illustrations are created rather than reproduced. With illustrations, advertisers can take a more analytical approach—by presenting charts and graphs—or a lighter approach, by creating characters to represent the product.

When smaller visuals are needed—especially those inserted into copy blocks—illustrations, like line art, reproduce better than photographs do. Because in newspaper we are striving for a stark black-and-white image as opposed to a grayed-down photographic image, illustrations and line art stand out on a gray page, help to retain white space, and emphasize blacks.

Clip or Stock Art

Using either clip art or stock art is a great option when money is tight. **Clip art** is a line-art drawing. **Stock art** is existing photographs of all varieties that can be purchased and used. These terms are often used interchangeably. The only problem with using clip or stock art is the small chance that you may see it in someone else's ad. To make your clip or stock art more unique, try combining one or more photos and removing or cropping unwanted areas.

GRAPHICS

Consistency is vital to recognition. Design should not test the creative waters at random. A client's advertising should be recognizable to regular customers, even if the logo were removed. Tone of voice, type, and layout style are some options that designers use to individualize a graphic style.

Borders

To confine or not to confine? That's the question when deciding whether to design a border for your ad. It's not a required design element, but a border can help in calling attention to your ad on the page. Borders are often used as a decorative element, tying an ad together and setting it off from surrounding copy. Borders can also be used inside an ad, around photographs or callout boxes to emphasize an image or any copy points that require special notice. By placing a drop shadow around one of these boxes, you can give it a three-dimensional feel, emphasizing it further.

Borders define the dimensions or edges of a newspaper ad. They can be fat, thin, double, or decorative. They should not interfere with the sales message or visuals. Many borders will feature cutesy graphic or illustrative

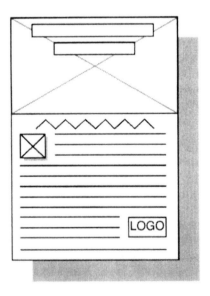

Drop shadows make photographs placed in insets appear to pop off of the page.

This napkin works as a border to frame the silverware.

borders. Using too many of these irrelevant images interferes with the message and steals much-needed white space. Less is more.

Borders should reflect the overall design of the ad. If your ad needs white space, create more by eliminating the border. Good judgment should be used when deciding to border or not to border. Design dictates.

When and How to Use a Border

For high-end stores and merchandise, use a thin or elegant-looking border. For discount establishments, a heavier border will do the trick. A good rule of thumb suggests that the overall weight of your border should reflect the weight of your typeface.

Borders need not be consistent in size. Consider making the top and bottom slightly thicker than the sides. This disperses the weight away from the center of the ad, creating the illusion of additional white space and making the ad appear larger.

An example with top and bottom borders
that are thicker than the side borders.

HOW MUCH DOES IT COST?

Cost is a very important question in consumers' minds. Letting them know
how much an advertised item costs is of utmost importance in retail design. Scream it out, make it large, make it bold or italicize it—just make
it a point to include the cost. There are many ways to show prices. Layout
style, type choices, and overall design will dictate look and placement.

Prices can appear in headlines or subheads, but they are usually located near descriptive copy blocks or wrapped within copy blocks describing the product. Often prices are shown with **superior** dollar or cent signs.
These are numbers or symbols set at least half the size of the price. Using
superiors with your prices, rather than having all numbers and/or symbols
the same size, presents a more sophisticated feel and creates white space.

PRICING

Prices are critical to effective newspaper advertising. They allow the consumer to compare prices, making the buying decision quicker and easier.

Prices can be displayed in many different ways. Examples taken from *The Design of Advertising* by Roy Paul Nelson.

However, known high-dollar products often eliminate price and entice the reader through copy by promoting benefits, image, and a special sale or financing to make purchasing easier.

As a rule, you should not shy away from displaying price. Make it big, make it bold, and give it class. Let it stand alone or tie it to a copy point. It doesn't matter where it appears, as long as it's there and readable.

IS THERE ANYTHING WRONG WITH NEWSPAPER ADVERTISING?

Yes, newspaper advertising has some problems, but they are few. Newspaper is a mass media vehicle, and it takes a kind of kneel-and-pray approach to reaching its potential target market. Advertisers attempt to counter this difficulty by placing their ads in the appropriate special sections offered by newspapers, such as sports, business, or lifestyle.

The worst problem is the paper stock. The uncoated, inexpensive newsprint causes the ink to bleed, which affects the printing quality. Life span is also a big problem; newspapers are old within twenty-four hours.

WHY USE NEWSPAPER?

Newspaper advertising reaches a lot of people, is effective, offers flexible deadlines, and is relatively inexpensive. Since ads normally arrive at the newspaper complete, deadlines of twenty-four hours or less can still make the next day's edition.

Newspapers are read not only for news value, but for the news of advertising; it's where people look for information about sales. It should inspire the consumer to want and/or need the product or service being advertised right now. To do this, price and product description play a prominent role. Retail advertising's only job is to make a sale. One way to accomplish this is by instilling a sense of urgency, through such devices as limited time offers, limited quantities, two-for-one offers, special sale hours, preferred customer sales, and coupons.

THE SALE

Everybody loves a sale. They are abundant in retail, and they promote predictable themes. The key is to decide how your client's sale will be unique, and then grab the reader—preferably by the throat. To do this, your team must first do a little brainstorming. What will be unique, fun, or unusual about the sale? Headlines, subheads, visuals, and typeface choices all need to reflect the sale's theme.

Sales should not seem routine. The personality of the sale should reflect that of the product or store. Sales create traffic within a store, and traffic promotes additional purchases. Most sales events are associated with holidays, special events, and overstocks, but why limit yourself? Be creative with your sales. Why not have a sale called "It's Tuesday. Let's Shop Till We Drop Together"?

TYPE AND IMAGE

The choice of typeface should reflect a product or company's personality. Type is not a whimsical or temporary choice. Once a typeface is chosen, it should appear in every ad—no matter what the media vehicle. The typeface should become a representative device for that product or service. Type is an art form of shapes, curves, circles, and lines. Making these elements your own, and thus your client's, is an extension of the graphic process. Remember to limit the number of typefaces to no more than two or three; less is desirable. To create variety, consider using multiple weights or even italics for emphasis. An ad's layout as well as type choice should also reflect your target market. Bigger type and less formal layouts work well when attracting younger consumers; whereas cleaner, more structured layouts work well in attracting older consumers.

CLUTTER

Retail ads have a lot to say and show in a small space. Clutter and chaos are not the designer's ultimate goal. A good designer organizes elements to control the structure of the ad. If you think of the elements being grouped as geometric shapes, order will replace chaos as you stack and arrange your block of shapes. To create elegance and order, to stress quality over price, use white space liberally; and stay away from bold or bulky typefaces. Consider using serif type, which is more sophisticated. For a more disciplined look, consider using lightweight sans serif faces.

Too many products? Consider grouping them together in a relevant setting.

Coupons need not spoil a great design.

Coupons

All consumers like to get a break; coupons are a way to offer them something in return for their patronage and loyalty, or as an introduction to your product or service. A coupon is an effective, temporary sales device. It should be easy to remove from the ad, and it should clearly point out the offer. When two or more coupons are used in an ad, a consistent look is very important. Here are some elements to consider when designing a coupon:

1. Size of the coupon may vary, it usually depends on how many coupons will be appearing in the ad. One thing is for sure; they should never be the size of a postage stamp.

2. The headline should clearly state the offer. Example: "Buy One Taco Burrito Platter and Get a Second Free."
3. If the offer is a cents-off or a percentage-off deal, use a larger typeface and point size to make it stand out.
4. If the offer can be redeemed at the local grocer, then a small amount of body copy is needed to tell the grocer how to redeem the used coupons.
5. Grocer's coupons also need to have a unit product code (UPC)— those thick-to-thin vertical lines used to ring up purchases by swiping the code across a computer beam.
6. Don't forget the product or store logo. The first thing the consumer does with a coupon is to tear it off the original ad in order to redeem it. They need to know where to go after removing the coupon.
7. Most coupons have an expiration date. This time limit should be prominently displayed, either at the top of the coupon or in bold or italic type in the body of the coupon.
8. If the product comes in more than one size or flavor, or any other variation that might cause confusion for the consumer, add a picture of the product to make buying the correct item easier.
9. Coupons may also include a marketing code. This code tells the retailer where the coupon came from, assisting with future media placement.

Designing Coupons

As mentioned earlier, the design of multiple coupons must be consistent. Headlines need to stay the same size, as do percentages or cents-off claims, on every coupon. Alternative type sizes can be used when heads are not of the same length, structure, or consistency. For example, suppose you are working with three coupons. Two of them have fairly long headlines that will break into three lines; the third has a short headline, only two lines long. Consider placing the two coupons with long headlines at each end of the lineup, and the one with the shorter headline in the middle. Continuity is maintained without altering type size. All headlines, price points, visuals, expiration dates, and logos should appear in the same place and be the same size on each coupon. Consider placing a dashed line around your coupon to visually encourage the consumer to cut or tear it out.

Where Should the Coupons Go?

Deciding where the coupons should go is another one of those great questions. Although there's no rule, you'll want to consider how easily the coupon can be removed. Coupons can appear aligned at the top of an ad; vertically down either side; or, most often, at the bottom of the ad. Placing a coupon in the center of the design should be avoided in newspaper advertisements. However, as with all design "shoulds" and "should-nots," design and concept should dictate.

FREESTANDING INSERTS

Freestanding inserts, or **FSIs**, are one-page, full-color ads that are inserted into the newspaper. Printed on a coated or treated paper stock, these inserts can be double-sided and usually feature coupons or announce a special sale or promotion. Sizes range, but FSIs are most often $8\frac{1}{2} \times 11$ inches. These nationally distributed inserts are also known as **supplemental advertising.**

CHAPTER SEVEN

A Look at Each Component as a Design Element

It is past time to bring yourself into a new era.

The Zurvan, a combination of a watch and TV, is on sale now at JC-Penny for $1600.

SONY

WHICH LAYOUT STYLES WORK BEST IN NEWSPAPER? WHICH DON'T?

Almost all layout styles can effectively showcase your product or service. However, the most successful are big type, silhouette, frame, picture window, and rebus.

Big Type

Big type never fails in newspaper ads. The bold solid black headlines create large black areas that are very eye-catching. Remember that a newspaper page appears gray to the human eye. Not only does your eye notice

Big type.

large areas of black and white, but your peripheral vision also notices these areas.

Big type can be used with smaller grouped visuals. These visuals should support the headline. Use big type only when you have something clever or important to say. Remember, a headline's job is to stop attention. So if you've got the targets' attention, say something beneficial to them. Since most visuals appearing in this layout style are small, consider using line art to maintain details.

Circus

The circus layout is all too common in newspaper advertising. I shudder even to suggest you consider its use, *ever.* With all the "events" taking

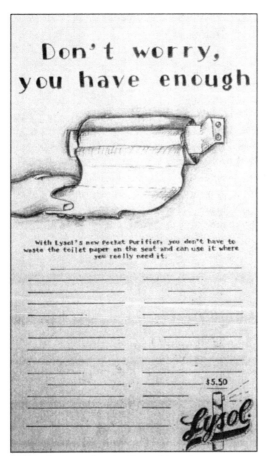

A simple frame border for a tidy ad.

place in a circus layout, it is difficult to maintain your product's dignity. Recall that circus layouts feature not only multiple products and multiple typefaces and sizes but also bursts and seasonal illustrations of all kinds. If you must indulge, build a good structural foundation for eye flow, and create white space. Begin by controlling the items that you can, and group the products. Think of the page as made up of squares and rectangles moving both horizontally and vertically, and group related items.

Copy Heavy

Copy-heavy ads are inadvisable for newspaper ads, for obvious reasons. Retail ads should make the sell at a glance; little or no effort should be required on the consumer's part. Copy-heavy ads blend in with the rest of the gray on a copy-heavy page. Without strong black-and-white contrasts and lacking a dominant image, your client's ad can easily be overlooked on the crowded newspaper page.

Frame

Most newspaper ads have a frame or border around them. The dimensions of the frame specify the size of the ad. Adding a frame to newspaper ads helps separate them from the rest of the print on the page. No matter which frame design or thickness you choose, the frame should match the store, product, or client image.

A frame's size depends on how much you want it to stand out from, or blend into, the design. The size of a frame is determined in points. This is a holdover from the days of technical pens, when line size was deter-

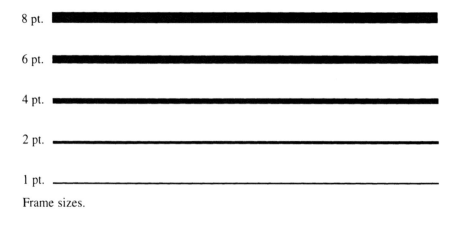

Frame sizes.

Mondrian example.

mined by the pen tip you used. Some of the most commonly used frame sizes appear on page 102.

Fancy or froufrou borders must be used with care. They are distracting and make an ad look smaller, diminishing the appearance of white space. Detailed borders can also fill in and lose their distinctiveness due to bleed on the page.

Mondrian

The Mondrian layout can be used in newspaper. However, its strength is its ability to use bright and multiple colors. But nothing says you can't give it a try with solid black typefaces, multiple gray tints, and line art or illustrations.

Multipanel

Due to the need to have small captions underneath each panel, the multi-panel layout style does not reproduce well. Thus, it does not project your design with strength.

Picture window with inset.

Picture Window

Picture-window layouts work best when showing people, food, land-scapes, and so forth. They feature a headline that overprints the visual and invites the consumer into the photograph.

Photographs in newspaper should include strong black-and-white contrasts to counter the tendency to bleed to flat grays. Too many grays will cause a greater loss of detail when reproduced on newsprint.

Headlines that appear within the photograph should be either reversed out or placed in the lightest area of the photograph—against sky, water, or a wall. Type should be bold and solid black to ensure readability and legibility.

Picture-window photographs usually stretch to the border; they do not overlap the border, but butt up against it. This type of layout lends itself well to having an additional smaller photograph placed elsewhere in the ad. Usually placement occurs within the body copy or as an inset. These

Rebus example.

inserts often have a border around them (either black or white), and they can show a more detailed shot of the product or give specific product points all in one convenient place. These inserts are often placed in the lower right-hand corner, over the larger or main photograph.

Rebus

Rebus layouts allow for the use of multiple visuals. These visuals are of varying sizes and are often found in descriptive copy. This is a great time to consider the use of illustrations or line art since the visuals will be relatively small.

You might include a large picture of a spokesperson, a medium-sized

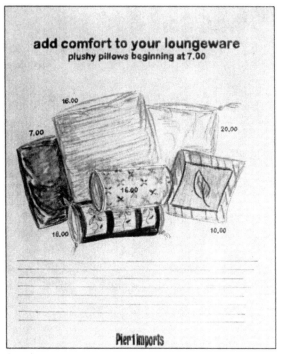

Silhouette example.

picture of the product in use, and then smaller visuals showing optional uses or assembly.

Silhouette

The grouping of multiple products, as discussed earlier, is a great attention getter. The target can picture how the items will look in her home. Better yet, if your client is selling linens or comforters, show the product on a bed. If your client sells small tables, pillows, sheets, pictures, or curtains, add those to the visual. You might be surprised at the number of people who do not know how to decorate. Many of them will buy more products just to match what was shown in the ad.

Silhouettes in newspaper work best when using illustrations or line art. Details can be lost or even blend together in a photograph on newsprint. Details can be highlighted in an illustration.

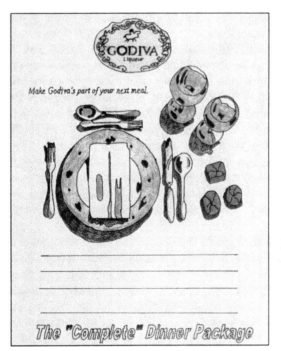

Showing the consumer how to use the product
educates and can also prompt additional sales.

ANYTHING GOES IF IT'S DONE WELL

The great thing about design is that nothing is impossible, especially if
your concept is strong and the ad can be read easily and quickly understood.

Any design taboos can be outdesigned with great success in any layout
style or format. The key is in knowing both the ups and downs of print
production before choosing a course of design action.

Ads with Multiple Elements

Ads with too many elements are the most common problem found in
newspaper design. A designer must decide what to do with fifteen product
items, a headline, descriptive copy, grand opening announcements, maps,
store hours, addresses, phone numbers, and logos. It's too much in too
little space. This has always been a problem without a firm solution. The

best place to start is by arranging the pieces in order of their importance and relationships.

Creating relationships allows you multiple alternatives when considering how to group things. Most ads have a point or reason for their creation, such as to advertise a linen sale, silver sale, or patio sale. Advertising multiple pieces of linen is one of the easiest design problems to solve. Consider stacking items; if different prices or fabrics are featured, use callouts beside the item with a description and/or price. If you can give one specific price or a range of prices, use the headline or subhead. Descriptive points can then be placed in the accompanying body copy. You might also consider stacking items like office products—anything goes, from paper to desks. Stacking creates a beautiful vertical line that matches the vertical shape of most newspaper ads. Irregular shapes create eye appeal.

If you're selling china or silver, add a table and create a place or table setting. Again, callouts help organization. A newspaper ad's job is to make a sale; if you can do it by showing additional items, all the better.

If for some reason you end up with a hodgepodge sale, consider using one large visual and headline together at the top of the page, and placing smaller items into a grid below. Placing one item in each grid square creates a sense of order. Each grid should contain a small headline, usually telling what the product is; a small amount of body copy, describing the item; and prices, if applicable for each item. In newspaper design, prices should either be large or set off in a bold typeface. If there are just too many visuals to confine to a grid, consider an anomaly-style layout where your product is the misfit within a set pattern. Controlling eye flow, structure, and balance are the keys to creating clean, readable, and legible newspaper ads.

TYPE AND NEWSPRINT

When you're choosing type for a newspaper ad, it is important to keep in mind the type design and the quality of paper on which your ad will be printed. Newsprint is what's considered an uncoated paper stock. That means the paper has no coating to keep the ink from bleeding. Since newsprint has a high bleed spread, it is important to choose typefaces that can withstand this kind of abuse and still be readable and legible.

GENERATIONS OF TYPE

Type quality is affected by the numerous stages leading up to printing. When you send your disc to the printer, this is generation one, or its teen

Bb Bb Bb B

Type becomes difficult to read when pieces of it
"fall out" during printing, affecting readability.
Be sure to select a typeface that will hold up on
coarse or textured paper stocks.

years. The printer will then pull, or shoot, a full-size negative of your ad; this is generation two, or middle age. That negative is then burned into printing plates, creating generation number three, or the retirement years. With each generation, the quality of the type deteriorates more. It ages and begins to fall apart.

Choosing a serif typeface whose letterforms go from thick to thin is risky; the thin areas can "fall out" during printing. Once parts of your typeface disappear, readability and legibility are affected.

So if you're choosing a serif face for newspaper, be sure it's at the slightly bulkier end of the spectrum. Sans serif typefaces always work great in newspaper; they are tough enough, and often fat enough, to withstand multiple generations of printing.

You Can Believe in Photographs

Photographs are believable. They are also expensive. The decision to include a photograph instead of an illustration or line art depends on the concept being used, the image of the product or service, and the medium.

The Photo Shoot

At a photo shoot, the photographer, the art director, the account executive, and often the client all get together to photograph the product. Photo shoots are expensive. You are paying for time, equipment, and the reputation of the photographer. Depending on the product and number of photographs needed, a photo shoot can take anywhere from a couple of hours to a couple of days.

If you're working with food, you will also need the assistance of a good stylist. These are the people who painstakingly work at making apples shinier, hamburgers juicier, and vegetables fresher.

Photo shoots are most commonly done after the client has approved layouts. In preparing the shoot, the photographer, with the art director's assistance, arranges and rearranges the products in groups, as shown on the rough or super comp. To match the grouping to the rough, props are often required. It is not uncommon to use such things as bricks, duct tape, string, wire, and assorted rags and towels to get a desired result, none of which will show in the final photographs.

Lighting is also very important during a photo shoot. Noting where highlights should appear, and where shadows need to be added or removed, is important. These things need to be looked at and considered during the shoot. Even though lighting issues can be corrected on the computer, your client will have to pay for the extra time it takes to retouch the photograph(s).

At the time of the shoot, it is also important that the photographer know the final photo size and the medium in which it will be used. For newspaper advertising, nine out of ten shoots will be done in black and white.

REPRODUCTION ISSUES

Once the photo shoot and any photo retouching are completed, it is time to think about getting the photograph(s) scanned into the computer and ready for printing.

Resolution: The Square-to-Dot Process

Resolution is the amount of detail that will appear in the printed piece. Resolution is determined during the scanning of photographs into the computer, and it refers to the size the pixel needs to be in order to reproduce the image on the computer screen. **Pixels** are a series of small colored or gray-tinted squares that create the photo's image and/or color variations on the computer screen.

As the designer, the first thing you need to consider is what size or resolution these pixels need to be. But before you can do that, you need to know where the piece is going to be used.

Professional printers do not deal in resolution; they deal in line screens. In printing, resolution is determined by the size of the line screen that is used to reproduce the ad in the newspaper or magazine. Printers also do not deal in pixels; they deal with a dot pattern, or the line screen, in order to reproduce photographs or illustrations.

Line screens come in various sizes—anywhere from 55 to 300 lines per inch (lpi). A line screen is made up of thousands of lines of dots. The smaller the line screen number, the larger and farther apart the dots will be; so the line screen accommodates for bleed on uncoated paper stocks.

A line screen replaces the pixels needed to reproduce photographs on a computer screen with the dot pattern needed to reproduce an image during printing.

The larger the dot, the better the reproduction on newsprint. The line screen number refers not only to the dot size but also to the quality of the paper on which the newspaper is printed. An 85-line screen means the paper stock is of a higher quality than one that uses a 65-line screen. Higher-quality newsprint is usually whiter in color and produces less bleed, allowing for the use of a smaller line screen.

Resolution, as determined by pixels, must be able to convert to the proper line screen (lpi). For example, suppose you are working on a newspaper ad that will run in the local paper, which uses a 65-line screen. This line screen number tells you that the dots are relatively large; you can see them with the naked eye, and they are spaced far enough apart so that when printed on newsprint, each dot can bleed up and touch one another without overlapping. You have probably noticed these dots in newspaper photographs. If the wrong line screen is used, you will know it; the bleed overlap makes for a muddy-looking photograph.

A black-and-white photograph that already has a dot pattern is called a *halftone* photograph. No black-and-white photograph is printed without first being converted into a black-and-white halftone.

The tough part is that resolution during the computer scanning process does not match the line screens used in printing. So what should you do? Art directors and printers recommend a resolution of 150 for newspaper ads using a 65- to 85-line screen. A resolution of 300 is recommended for magazine ads using a 133-line screen.

The official formula suggests that if a 65-line screen is used, then the resolution would be one and a half times the line screen number: $65 \times 1.5 = 97.5$. For a 133-line screen, the resolution would be two times the line screen number: $133 \times 2 = 266$. The results aren't exact, so you will have to round up to the nearest available resolution.

Just a Pinch of Color: To Have or Not to Have?

Color stands out in stark contrast to the standard black-and-white newspaper page. Once you add color, you add cost—a lot more cost. Color usually appears on the back page in newspaper; however, that need not be the rule. If color is not a viable option, consider using screen tints or duotones.

Shades or Screen Tints

Tonal areas can range from very light to medium to dark to very dark, and they can be created from any solid color. These tones are known as **screen tints** in printing and **shades** in desktop publishing. For example, solid black is 100 percent of saturation, or a solid color. A 10-percent screen of black would give you a light-gray tint, a 40-percent screen of black would give you a medium gray, and so on.

I always tell my students to think about it like this: If you're holding a black pencil and you color lightly, exerting little pressure on the pencil point, you get a light-gray color. The harder you push, the darker and more diverse the tones become. The addition of tones gives a black-and-white ad in particular a more three-dimensional appearance, creating foregrounds and backgrounds.

This design option is great for callout boxes, drop shadows, snipes, banners, backgrounds, and line-art accents. Screen tints should not be used on type, because they would drastically affect readability and legibility.

Duotones

Duotone means two colors, usually black plus another color. The second color, which is usually a Pantone Matching System (PMS) color or a specific color choice, is added to a black-and-white photograph. In a duotone the second color attaches itself to the light-colored or tonal areas of the photograph, giving it a faux full-color feel. Duotones are not used often enough. They would certainly attract attention, and they are about half the price of a full-color ad. Dutones are an inexpensive way to get noticeable results.

GRAPHIC ELEMENTS

If the goal is to make your ad stand out on the page, then the addition of graphic design elements can only further that goal. **Graphics** can be defined as additional devices such as grids, bars, and boxes that add dimension and/or organization to an ad. Graphics can also include dashed lines for coupons, arrows, snipes, and bursts. Don't forget about type.

Boxes, Bars, and Lines

If you are using several smaller photographs or illustrations in your design, consider placing them within a ruled box. This minor graphic addition

In this example, a fine graphic line is used between columns to create a more elegant and structured look.

gives the visuals a definitive start and stop, pulling the eye toward the center of action. Using black bars to define the top and bottom of an ad or to highlight important information creates additional strong blacks on the page. Fine ruled lines can also be used to separate copy from photographs.

Type as a Design Element

The typeface you choose should reflect the personality of the product or ambience of the service or store. The openness or tightness of line- and letterspacing can promote this personality further, creating a signature look for the product or service.

Work with type; make it your own, and in turn your client's. Never settle for what the computer can do; design the type, and make the computer do what you want the type to do.

SIZE SPECIFICATIONS

Newspaper space is measured from side to side in **column inches,** or the width of a column of typeset copy plus the gutter. The depth of an ad is measured in quarter-inch increments, up to twenty-one inches. While the newspaper works within predetermined widths, the depth of an ad is deter-

mined by design and budget constraints. The following are choices for
column widths:

1 column	$2^{1}/_{16}$ inches
2 columns	$4^{1}/_{4}$ inches
3 columns	$6^{7}/_{16}$ inches
4 columns	$8^{5}/_{8}$ inches
5 columns	$10^{13}/_{16}$ inches
6 columns	13 inches

A full-page ad measures 13 column inches wide by 21 inches deep.

It's important to get the size right. If the ad does not fit, the newspaper
will automatically reduce it. As the designer, you do not want that to happen. Quality is affected by resizing, which creates an additional generation. This kind of mistake should be avoided at all costs, since reduction
also affects line screens.

CHAPTER EIGHT

PUTTING THE PIECES IN PLACE

Is the Ad Okay?

The approval process is always tough on creatives. Once the ad is designed, it must go to the client for approval before any photo shoots or preparation for printing begin. Clients complete the approval process by signing off on concept, copy, and overall appearance of the ad or ads. If everything is good to go, which it never is, the client will sign off on the idea and preparation for printing can begin.

Your odds of winning the lottery are about as good as those of an ad's being approved without additional changes. Some changes are small; others are major and require a great deal of work to accomplish. Unfortunately, what never changes is the printing or publication deadline. All changes must be made immediately, no matter how big or small; the revised ad is then resubmitted to the client before going to the printer. Jobs are lost if deadlines are missed for either printing or insertion dates for

Anomaly. This ad also represents a well-balanced asymmetrical layout.

magazine or newspapers. A lot of money is at stake. Missing a deadline is like throwing money down the drain. Occasionally, but rarely, missed deadlines are the client's fault.

GETTING AN AD PRINTED

Very few bells, whistles, or complications are associated with preparing a newspaper ad for printing. Desktop publishing software—such as Quark, PageMaker, or InDesign—makes the job easy.

In advertising, most photo retouching work is done by professional photographers; so little photo work is required beyond sizing and cropping. If you work for a smaller agency, then the Adobe Photoshop software will help you with the retouching process.

When scanning photographs, designers must determine a resolution compatible with the line screen used by the newspaper. Desktop publishing software is used to assemble all elements of the ad, basically reproducing your rough on-screen. All photographs are placed, sized, and cropped in position within the layout and appear on-screen as low-resolution versions of the original photograph. At the printer, a halftone photograph replaces the scanned or low-resolution image.

File formats for photographs are chosen during the assembly stage. Most photographs coming from Photoshop into Quark should be saved as a TIFF (tagged information file format) file. Any work coming from Adobe Illustrator should be saved as an EPS (Encapsulated PostScript) file. The production stage is much more complicated and diverse than indicated in this discussion, but you'll find that the TIFF and EPS file formats satisfy most newspaper and magazine requirements.

USING A PRINTER

The term *printers* as used in this section refers to two different aspects of the production process. First there is the human printer, who is in charge of pulling negatives, producing plates, and assembling final photographs, to name just a few of his jobs. Then there is the actual printing machine. Now, I am not talking about the small printer that sits on your desk. I am talking about professional printers. These things are huge; some can fill up a large classroom. These printers have the capacity to print in both black and white and color, and they can produce large volumes at a time.

The human printer will replace all low-resolution photographs with halftone photographs, and he will pull or shoot negatives of your ad. These negatives are shot full-size, or to match the size of your ad. No small 35mm negatives are used during professional printing.

Next, human printers assemble the negatives as they will appear on the newspaper page, and then they create the printing plates. A **printing plate** is a thin metal sheet, flexible enough to wrap around a large printing drum. The negative is etched into the plate, which is used in the printing process. The plates work like a big rubber stamp, reproducing the ad by transferring ink to paper.

SOME DISASTERS

Most of the following issues have been discussed or mentioned in previous chapters, but let's take one more look.

Newsprint is not an optimal printing surface. The coarse, uncoated, highly bleedable stock affects print quality and color reproduction. Photographs can look flat, and delicate illustrations and typefaces can literally disappear off the newsprint's surface during printing. Choices made when designing help to alleviate this fault. Things to consider are type size, design, and weight. Make sure your type is not too dainty, and that it does not go from a thick to thin style, to keep it from breaking up and "falling out." Small type that is too bold will bleed together, also affecting readability and legibility. The same holds true if type is set too close together. Overall, it is advisable to avoid using decorative or delicate typefaces, choosing instead the plainer, more streamlined faces.

Consider using solidly drawn illustrations or line art, instead of grayed-down photographs, to show more detail and to create strong black-and-white contrasts on the page. Black-and-white line art, due to its absence of tones, doesn't need a dot pattern in order to be reproduced. Line screens are required only for photographs, both black and white and color, or for illustrations that are made up of varying tones.

Limitations of Photographs

Photographs can become flat and details suffer on newsprint. The large dot pattern needed to reproduce photographs makes details look like broken pieces of pottery. Color is muted and grainy, leaving the ad flat and muddy looking.

The Rock and the Hard Place

No discussion of disasters would be complete without talking about missed deadlines. Outside of printing, the only disasters I have ever encountered in advertising are missed deadlines. In short, they can't happen. If on some rare occasion a deadline is missed, I guarantee that someone will be out of a job by the end of the day. Deadlines are fixed and nonnegotiable. Missed deadlines mean lost revenue for the client.

Some Positives

All negatives can be turned into positives by understanding print production and how it affects design decisions.

If the quality of newsprint is poor, design more simply, adjust type choices, keep body copy to a minimum, work with large elements, and consider using illustrations or line art rather than photographs. Line art helps your ad to stand out on the page, as well as highlighting and defining details better than photographs.

Type Size

Keep your type big and sturdy. Large type creates large, rectangular blocks of black on the page. Just the opposite happens when headlines and subheads are smaller; they create an excess of white space. Either option can produce positive results. Body copy should be kept to a minimum. Highlight only what you want the target to do, and include enough about the product to seduce the reader into action. Remember, in retail we want consumers to act, to get up and visit the store, or to make a toll-free call and place an order. Newspaper advertising is not meant to educate through the use of large blocks of copy; instead, it entices.

Uncoated Paper Stocks

Uncoated paper is inexpensive. It can be bought in large quantities, used, and then thrown out. Because of this, newspaper space can be purchased fairly inexpensively. It can reach a mass audience on a daily basis, making it a very attractive medium.

Getting It There

Newspapers have very short deadlines. This allows for last-minute ads, or a second chance to make changes to an existing ad, up until twenty-four hours prior to printing.

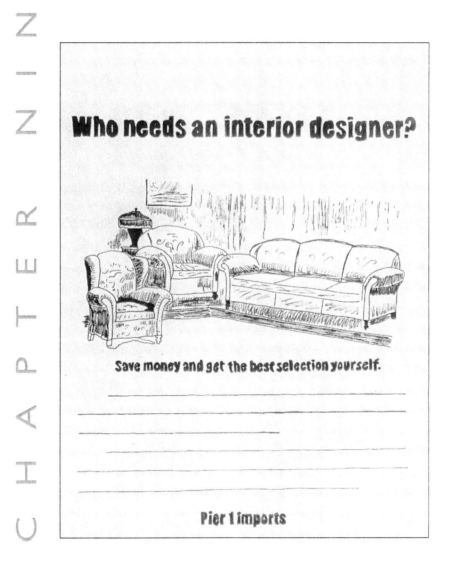

Thinking in words is what we have been trained to do all our lives. Learning to visualize what those words mean is a little trickier. I find that young designers often have trouble explaining why they chose to do something; that is, why did you choose that concept direction, typeface, or layout style? Everything has a purpose in design. All decisions are based on a thought, an event, or a passing cloud. Coworkers and clients alike want to know what you were thinking when designing. This helps them not only to understand the concept, but how the target might view the idea.

Let's put the skills and information learned in the previous chapters to work in the following exercises. You will have a chance to do a little brainstorming, create a word list, and design a newspaper ad or two.

EXERCISE LEVEL ONE: BRAINSTORMING

Break up into groups of two or three and come up with three concept pitches for the product or service assigned in class. Create a word list to help with the visual/verbal process. Present your group's ideas to the class.

EXERCISE LEVEL TWO: WORD LIST

Don't get caught up in the excitement of one good idea, whether it relates to the unique selling proposition (USP) or big idea or not. Writing out ideas and concepts both visually and verbally helps you not only with understanding your assignment but also with understanding the why of message development. Begin the design process by creating a word list of 20–25 words to get the creative juices flowing for the product presented in class, and then fill out the following Think Sheet. Next, present your preliminary ideas to the class, or work in teams combining ideas. Be able to back up your decisions. This exercise can be completed by working in groups or individually depending on class assignment.

EXERCISE LEVEL THREE: THUMBNAILS

In this exercise, you'll begin to visually execute your word list and Think Sheet. Create twenty thumbnails from your best concept development ideas. Be sure each thumb is different; do not reuse heads, subheads, or visuals. Try as many different layout styles as you can. Think of the trade-offs regarding redundancy versus diversity. If you do not offer diversity when presenting your ideas, you run the risk of your client hating the few ideas you have. It will be back to the drawing board—or worse yet, a lost

Think Sheet: Solving an Advertising Problem

1. What is your USP or big idea?
2. What are the strongest benefits and features of your products/service?
3. What is your concept?
4. How will your concept assist consumers in imagining themselves in, or using, the product?
5. What type(s) of approach will you use? Explain.
6. What layout solutions will you use for this client, and why? Explain.
7. Will you use photographs, illustrations, graphic designs, or line art to promote the product? Explain your choices.
8. What typeface will fit the concept or personality/image of the product or service? Explain.
9. What should be the dominant element?
10. What retail devices will aid in creating action on the part of the consumer? For newspaper design only.
11. Will you be using any announcement devices like snipes, bursts, or banners? Explain. For newspaper design only.
12. What layout style(s) are you considering for use? Explain.
13. Will you design around an existing tagline or slogan, or will you create a new one? Explain.
14. Will you use a spokesman or create a character for your product or service? Explain.

new business pitch. Present your individual group's thumbnails to the class or instructor. Final rough size 3 columns × 10½ inches.

EXERCISE LEVEL FOUR: ROUGHS

Level four begins the rough stage. Choose three out of your twenty thumbnails that you will take to roughs. These thumbs may have been chosen by you, the class, or the instructor. The roughs should be very polished. Use references for visuals and type if your drawing skills need a little support. Offer three separate concept ideas. Present them to the class. Size: 3 columns × 10.5 inches.

CLASS CRITIQUES

Use the Think Sheet that you originally created to evaluate your concept. Hand out copies to the class. How many things had to change, and why?

What were some of the challenges you encountered? Compare and contrast, through discussion with your classmates, your successes and ultimate failures.

EVALUATION

Use the Project Evaluation Sheet at the end of this chapter for determining success and areas that still need work. The Project Evaluation Sheet has two important functions. First, it will be used by your instructor or classmates to determine your final grade. Secondly, it should be used by you as a self-evaluation tool to make sure you have successfully completed all aspects of the assignment.

EXERCISE LEVEL FIVE: DESIGN WITH MULTIPLE COUPONS

For this exercise, start the whole design process over from the beginning. This time, create an ad design with multiple coupons (two or three). Offer three versions of one concept idea. Size: 4 columns × 11 inches.

EXERCISE LEVEL SIX: REMINDER AD

Create a follow-up or reminder ad for the sales event created in level four. How will you keep interest alive? Match your strongest concept. Size: 2 columns × 10½ inches.

EXERCISE LEVEL SEVEN: DIFFERENT APPROACHES, SAME CONCEPT

In exercise level seven, you'll begin the whole process again. This time, instead of offering three separate concept ideas, develop three different approaches to the same concept. Present your approaches to the class. Size: 4 columns × 11 inches.

Project Evaluation Sheet

Stage of design to be graded:

General Project   Thumbnails   Roughs   Super Comps   Computer

Total points available on this project: _____

Total points earned this project: _____

Projects will be evaluated on the following:

1. Appropriateness of design: _____

2. Concept/Idea: _____

3. Use of shapes/illustrations (sources): _____

4. Use of typography: _____

5. Appropriate use of color: _____

6. Presentation of project: _____

7. Use of computer skills: _____

8. Directions were followed as assigned: _____

9. The USP or big idea was identifiable in the design: _____

10. During critique, the big idea or USP was clearly defined: _____

NOTE: Not all items will apply to each project.

Additional Comments:

MAGAZINE: WHAT'S THE BIG DESIGN DEAL?

What Is Magazine Advertising?

Selling a product, as in newspaper, is much easier when price and limited-time offers are all you really have to worry about.

Magazine advertising, on the other hand, concentrates on the creation of an image or mood through visual and verbal relationships. The advertising job is to entice the reader into the ad. To do this, the designer needs to create a conceptual environment that the reader can both relate to and experience through the words and visuals. The show-and-tell nature of magazine advertising allows products to speak for themselves and demonstrate results. Although diverse in nature, many products appearing in magazines are often exclusive or unique, and they are expensive to own. Other products are more mainstream, and their features may be indiscernible from the features of their competitors' products.

Products boasting higher price tags are less likely to be purchased on impulse. Before buying, the consumer will research a product's benefits and features, identify where the product fits into their own lives, and determine which problems it can solve. Information should be readily available to assist the consumer in making an informed buying decision.

The trendy shopper, on the other hand, uses magazine advertising to look at all the competing products within a category. With little to differentiate one brand of sneakers from another, product features take a backseat to how the consumer will look, feel, or be perceived in the sneakers.

When image and product features are prominent, price plays a more subordinate role in the design. The focus is placed instead on the benefits of owning or using a product or service; because of this, visuals tend to play a more dominant role, as does lengthy fact-based copy. By creating a strong visual/verbal relationship, you can tap into a reader's left- and right-brain tendencies by allowing the consumer to see the product being worn or used, to learn what colors and sizes are available, and to review safety information and warranties.

Print Design for Special-Interest Magazines

The more specialized the magazine, the more the advertising team knows about the consumer who will see their client's advertising. Dog lovers read dog magazines, car lovers read car magazines, and clothing lovers read fashion magazines. This kind of specialized readership challenges the advertising team to create an environment that allows readers to participate in the advertising based on personal experience; this specialized interest produces readers who are loyal and who regularly pick up their favorite magazine at the local newsstand.

Magazine advertising should be a visually stimulating and informative experience for readers. Visual images should develop an identity and create a visual personality for the product or service. Copy should take the reader on a fact-finding adventure. Product image and user image should be woven throughout this personalized visual/verbal relationship. The magazine's relationship with the consumer allows the advertising to talk directly to the people who will be buying and using the product(s).

Unlike newspapers, magazines have a long life span. Due to the highly individualized content of magazines, consumers tend to hold onto them longer, often trading with other enthusiasts or friends. This gives advertising a second chance to make a first impression and reach out to a larger portion of the target audience.

A magazine's editorial content plays an important role in the advertising that appears within its covers. For example, advertising found in a home decorating magazine will promote products such as barbecue grills, paint and wallpaper products, and furniture and carpeting as well as patio and pool items.

Concepts that address lifestyle directly address image. Full-color visuals and dynamic copy work in tandem to create the appropriate consumer response.

Photographs bring the product or service alive with enhanced details. Textures are magnified, emotions are highlighted, and colors pop off the page. Copy can be longer since readers selectively spend more time with a magazine than they do with a newspaper. Story lines or plots can be developed to promote uses, scientific studies, demonstrations, purchase options, and trends.

Graphic designs or colorful illustrations attract attention by showcasing interesting shapes and brilliant color variations. Design styles and color usage can re-create time periods and suggest liberal or conservative views. Bold, colorful graphics suggest youth and energy, while subdued colors reflect relaxation and stability.

Headlines with strong consumer benefits seduce the target by relating product benefits to image. By touching an emotional cord in your target, advertising can suggest uses and promote new age fads or renaissance revivals.

Copy should let the consumer know what the experience will be like when using or interacting with the product or service. Be descriptive; write to the senses and the emotions. There is no "buy now while supplies last" mentality, as touted in newspaper advertising. Magazine advertising makes you feel, taste, and smell the product. The impersonal sale, sale, sale, aspects of newspaper are gone.

By offering a toll-free number or website for ordering or obtaining additional information, you can make purchasing easier. Another successful enticement is to offer coupons or samples including lotions, CDs, or perfumes.

The varied concept approaches used in magazines must accomplish an action or promote the quest for additional research on the part of the consumer. Good action or educational devices might include encouraging test drives or comparison shopping. Testimonials also successfully create consumer involvement by evoking curiosity. Informational ads are great educational vehicles, as are recipes that accompany a food product. Emotional appeals, how-to ads, and product demonstrations all work well in magazine advertising.

For magazine advertising, the goal is to assist the consumer with their buying decision. It is true that many people are not good cooks, fashion mavens, or intuitive decorators. By showing additional compatible products in the ad, the designer can prompt additional sales as readers attempt to duplicate what they see in their own homes or offices.

Headlines can speak volumes. Be sure to have a visual element that complements the headline.

Before designing, take the time to study the special-interest direction of the magazine(s) your ads are to appear in. Look at the other ads and do the opposite, or do it with more individualistic or targeted appeal than other advertisers have used.

It's Worth the Paper It's Printed On

Setting the appropriate mood is made a little easier due to the clay-coated paper stocks on which magazines are printed. The clay-coated surface allows the ink to sit on top of the paper rather than soaking in, as with newspaper stock. Coated paper stocks have a shiny surface as opposed to the dull, uncoated appearance of newsprint. The results show patterns that are more detailed, food that looks tastier, and fashions that are more colorful.

The Variety of Magazines

There are basically three categories of magazines: consumer, business or trade, and farming. Each of these three categories is broken down significantly further into special interests, like fashion, sports, cars, hobbies, advertising, marketing, public relations, and so forth.

The more we know about the targets' interests, lifestyles, and general demographics, the better. Concept development designed to meet the special interests of the reader makes isolating a unique selling proposition (USP) or big idea easier.

Co-op Advertising

Co-op or **cooperative advertising** means that two individual but compatible clients have paired up to share the cost of the advertising and encourage consumers to use their products together. These highly successful partnerships might team an airline with a hotel chain to promote air and hotel packages to a destination accessed by both.

Other co-op ventures might include name-brand coffees served at national restaurant chains, or even computers that feature "Intel Inside."

What to Include and What to Avoid in Magazine Advertising

Since magazines sell an idea or an image of affluence, beauty, and even intellectual gadgets, prices should not be prominent in the advertising.

Informative copy with strong visual support.

Often these ads have no price at all, and little copy; they let the image sell the product. Consumers should be able to experience the benefits associated with the product or service and be encouraged to call, log onto, or visit their nearest retailer for more information.

The main thing to avoid in magazine design is clutter. The blending of type and photographs should create an elegant or classy, informative, playful, or imaginative appearance. Using abundant white space or even black-and-white photographs will set your ad off from most others in the magazine.

WHAT TO CONSIDER WHEN DESIGNING FOR MAGAZINE

Magazine sizes and printing requirements are relatively consistent. Magazines contain very few tacky or poorly designed ads, which could act to cheapen your product's appeal.

Ad sizes depend on the overall size of the magazine. The most com-

Multiple subheads enhance long copy by
breaking it up into smaller blocks.

mon full-size ad is around 8½ × 11 inches. Ad sizes range from one-third
of a page to a full page. Sizes vary per magazine, and they can be con-
firmed by consulting the SRDS (Standard Rate and Data Service). The
SRDS shows specific size guidelines for individual magazines, as well as
closing dates and bleed specifications.

Headlines and Subheads

Headlines should be informative and feature a strong consumer benefit
when possible. Remember, as designers we want the consumer to be able
to experience the product through our words and visuals. Headlines, unlike
those in newspaper, should not overpower the ad but blend in with the
ambiance created within the design. Garish is out; structure and informative class are in. Sizes for headlines vary in magazine ads; however, they
never scream loudly or are so loud and obese as to decrease the brand's
image or insult the educational or social level of the reader.

In magazines you can hold a reader's attention for a longer period of time, so headlines as well as body copy can be longer and more informative or instructive. Because of this, subheads are often not needed. However, if you have a great deal of body copy, you can use multiple subheads to break the ad into more pleasing and readable blocks. Think of them as chapter headings. A consumer can glance at the subheads and know what points will be stressed within the copy. If their interest has been aroused, they can decide either to read on or to come back later. Like headlines, subheads should not overpower but blend within the copy block. As far as style or format goes, these multiple subheads can be either a phrase or a complete sentence; design and copy content should dictate direction.

Body Copy

Body copy can be virtually nonexistent, short, medium, or long, depending on the message needing to be explained or introduced. The average ad has copy of medium length, just enough to continue the campaign theme and describe the product or service's attributes. Magazines often use a visual to do the talking for the copy. Good descriptive copy should spell out how the product works, what it sounds like, what it feels or smells like, and how much it weighs; it should also include a complete examination of benefits and uses. The consumer should be able to experience the product through your words.

Longer copy should set the scene in the same way the plot of a novel might. It should have a beginning, a middle, and an end, telling a story in detail. The beginning completes the USP or big idea that was introduced in the headline. The middle highlights product features, and the ending needs to tie the consumer benefits and features together and bring the copy to a natural climax; in our case, action.

THE ALLURE OF MAGAZINE DESIGN

Everything about designing for magazines is sexier and more exciting than designing for newspaper. Elite products allow the designer's fantasy world to come alive. The numerous products without an independent identity present a design challenge. Product individualism, or what sets your product off from the competition, is achieved through concept development, layout styles, and/or type choices.

It's important to point out that although these endless design possibilities appear to be tied to larger budgets, this is an illusion. Magazine advertising is indeed more expensive to produce than newspaper advertising. The better paper stocks and printing capabilities do improve quality and

Show-and-tell is one of the best ways to attract a
reader's attention.

influence design, but budgets big or small do not define design or great
creative. Great ideas rule advertising success, no matter what the budget.
There are no boring media vehicles or boring products; there are only
boring ideas.

GETTING IT THERE

Magazine deadlines or submission dates to publishers can provide designers anywhere from a few weeks to a couple of months, unlike the very
short deadlines associated with newspaper advertising.

Most newspapers are printed daily. Magazines have fewer publication
dates—ranging from weekly to biweekly, from monthly to bimonthly or
quarterly—making timely material almost impossible. Care needs to be
taken to think ahead not only about deadlines, but design content.

CHAPTER ELEVEN

A Look at Each Component as a Design Element

WHICH LAYOUT STYLES WORK BEST IN MAGAZINE?

Almost all layout styles work when designing for magazine, except for the cluttered circus-style layout. The choice of layout style depends on the concept and overall product image.

Copy Heavy

Because magazine ads can hold a reader longer, copy-heavy layout styles are well suited to this medium. Magazine ads inform. If you have a new or unusual product, or even a new use for an old product, lengthy and informative copy could become the dominant design element. The need to know is critical to the need to purchase.

Frame

This layout style is not often used in full-size magazine ads. Frames usually define the dimension, or ad size, and in magazine this usually means

A copy heavy example.

Frame. A unique way to isolate your message graphically.

the magazine size. This is problematic; when the magazine is trimmed down to size during printing, your border or frame will be cut off. Smaller magazine ads often use a frame to separate the ad from surrounding copy. Most often, borders in magazine design are used as graphic or decorative elements and need to be inset at least a half-inch on all four sides to avoid being cut off when the magazine is trimmed to size. White space can be used to frame the ad, or the background color can spread beyond the border to open up the ad. The use of borders should be considered carefully; they can make an ad look smaller and more confined. Frames should be designed to match the layout or type style, allowing for simple, unobtrusive lines or more illustrative, expressive lines.

Mondrian

The Mondrian layout style, with its colorful divisions and visual combinations, is ideally suited for magazine. Although controlling eye flow is not a strength of this layout style, by controlling visual size, color, and contrast, the designer can lead the consumer's eye to the largest photo or the

Mondrian example.

brightest color. Next to the colorful divisions, type stands out in stark black-and-white contrast to the controlled use of color and visual devises.

Multipanel

In magazine ads, the multipanel layout style works very well. Due to the quality of paper and printing, these multiple and often small and detailed panels work very well. They are especially effective when bringing an existing TV commercial to print. You can show the storyboard panels with more informational copy than a thirty- to sixty-second commercial will allow. This layout style is also great when showing product demonstrations or multiple uses.

Picture Window

Placing text atop a photograph invites the viewer to enter the photograph. A bench in the park allows viewers to imagine themselves enjoying an

Multipanel example.

afternoon of leisurely reading or people-watching. Remember, a magazine's job is to make readers experience the product through visual stimuli and descriptive copy. Invite them in.

Rebus

Copy that is longish in nature, and full of smaller drawings or even headlines that include visuals substituting for words, allows a rebus-style layout to tell a story by tying visuals literally into the copy. This style often features a larger photograph supported by a strong consumer benefit headline and additional photographs or illustrations that appear wrapped within or alongside the body copy. Copy will usually explain uses, present problem solutions, or even describe assembly.

Silhouette

Because it does not tend to show product use or demonstration, the silhouette layout style is not used as often in magazine layout as it is in newspa-

Picture window example.

Rebus example.

add style to your dinnerware
with fashion for your tabletop

Pier 1 imports

Silhouette example.

per. However, if you want a specific design or concept theme to be the focus, this layout style can bring the consumer in close.

Type Specimen

Although not used often enough to suit this author's tastes in magazines, the type specimen layout option says with type what cannot be shown with visuals. This layout style is a great teaser option if you want to announce the coming of a product but not show it, or feature single benefits. Nothing titillates more than tell and don't show. The choice of typeface and layout style will define the product's image—such as playful, elegant, or spirited.

TYPE AS A DESIGN ELEMENT

You can get a little fancier with type in magazine design, but readability and legibility continue to be important issues.

Type specimen example.

I certainly would not get any fancier than perhaps a script font. Anything more decorative edges toward tacky and garish, not to mention difficult to read. Ads may hold a reader's attention longer in magazine, but no one is going to take the time to stumble through an illegible headline text. If you must use a more decorative typeface, be sure it is set in either caps/lowercase or initial caps/lowercase, but never all caps.

The creative use of type is beautiful when it's arranged in an interesting way, emphasized with color, and has something important to say.

Serif typefaces can be tightly kerned (letterspaced), allowing the serifs to overlap more than might be allowed in newspaper design. Leading can also be tightened so letters from one line can connect with a letter from above or below, or fit snugly together like pieces of a puzzle. Kerning and leading issues become more critical as designing with type becomes a creative must.

Visuals that slightly overlap headline type work to tie the type and picture together. When type overlaps a photo, it should in fact overlap. Headline text should not just touch the photo, nor should the amount of

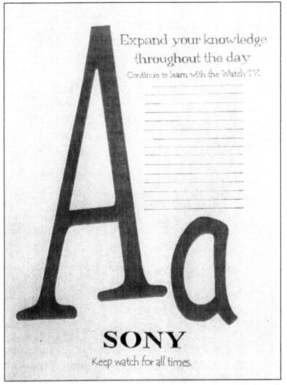

Type that plays a visual role can be very beautiful and interesting.

overlap affect readability. Consider starting at an overlap of one-eighth inch.

The decision whether to overlap depends on the typeface and weight used within the ad. Type that is too small or lightweight can be overwhelmed by a photograph that is too close. Other considerations include the headline itself. If the headline copy creates a visual/verbal relationship; for example, "Is This You?" and the visual shows a tired, worn-out working mother, then a direct relationship is formed between what is being said to what is being shown.

Body copy follows the same rules as in newspaper; 10- to 11-point copy with 1 point of leading is a great place to start and is the easiest to read. Using a common typeface, such as Times, makes readability and legibility easier still.

Obviously, the longer the copy, the smaller the type size will have to be. Go no smaller than 9-point type with 10-point leading. If you still can't

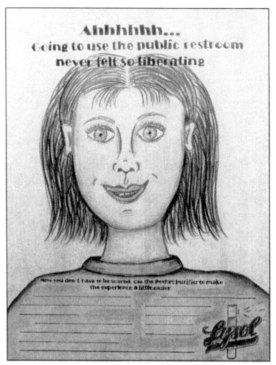

Type that overprints a photograph creates a visual/
verbal relationship.

fit all the copy, consider reducing the headline or visuals; or ask your
copywriter to edit the copy slightly.

Do not give up on including multiple subheads. Large gray areas of
type dull down even a magazine page. By adding bold or colorful subheads, you can break up long copy into pleasing, contrasting blocks.

THE IMAGE OF PHOTOGRAPHS

Photographs offer an exclusive viewing opportunity. Because of increased
quality and printing issues, the consumer can very clearly see what the
product looks like and/or how it is used.

Photographs bring reality home. As readers, we can see patterns, textures, quality, and color as if the product were sitting before us. The idea
of visual variety offers designers the option to include background or to
isolate the product or image by eliminating background clutter.

Photographs can be small or large; they can show the product alone or in use, placed in a relevant setting, or being compared to a similar product. Because magazines do not require a border, large photographs can bleed off the page. **Bleed** takes place when a photograph, illustration, background color, or graphic element extends at least one-eighth inch and up to one-quarter inch beyond the trim size, or the size of the ad on one or more sides. This means that once the magazine is trimmed down to size, the photograph or illustration will extend to the edge of the page; no white space will be showing on one or more sides. Bleed allows for more visual, but it is also more expensive.

Live, Trim, and Bleed

Magazine ads have three areas you need to be concerned with when designing: live, trim, and bleed. **Live area** in an ad measuring 8.5 × 11 inches would be around 7 × 10 inches. This is the area where type should be confined. Any kind of visual or graphic can extend beyond this area.

An example of a bleed photograph that dominates the layout.

The live area protects elements from being cut off when the magazine is trimmed.

The trim size is 8.5 × 11 for most full-size ads. The **trim** size reflects the ad size and the magazine size, and it is where the magazine will be trimmed during production.

Bleed extends beyond the trim. Any photograph that is designed to come up to the edge of the design must bleed beyond the trim size. Since the trimming of a magazine is not an exact science, bleed photographs not extending beyond the trim can leave little—but very noticeable—slivers of white space, or the page, showing around the edges of the ad. Very tacky.

It's important to find out if your client's budget can afford adding one or more bleed photographs. If it can, then the photographer must be made aware of all bleed shots during the photo shoot. If she comes in too close during shooting, there will not be enough photograph available to bleed later during production/printing.

RESOLUTION VERSUS LINE SCREEN

Since the paper stock used by magazines is a coated stock, the dot pattern or line screen can be much smaller and more compact. Coated paper stock allows little or no movement of ink on the page, enhancing print quality.

The most common line screen used in magazine contains 133 lines per inch (lpi). This means that the dot pattern is very small and closely spaced. As designers, we can use smaller line screens when bleed is not a major issue. When you're scanning a photograph into the computer, set the resolution at around 300 pixels per inch (ppi).

The most common photograph used in magazine is referred to as a **four-color** or **process color photograph.** All printed photographs must have a dot pattern or line screen in order to be reproduced. In newspaper the dot pattern is made up of black, white, and gray tones; in four-color photography, the dots are composed of concentrated percentages of cyan (C), magenta (M), yellow (Y), and black (K)—known as **CMYK.** Combinations of these four colors create all colors found in a color photograph.

To get a color photograph ready for printing, a four-color separation is prepared; it is made up of four negatives, one for each CMYK color. Tens of thousands of four-color dots are used to recreate a color photograph.

A 133-line screen is so fine that you cannot see these multicolored dots with the naked eye. But with a loop or magnifying glass, you can see the multitudes of CMYK dots making up any printed color photos.

Photographs are turned into four-color separations by professional color separators. However, Adobe Photoshop can also do it for you. But, as with photo retouching, four-color separations are best left to the experts.

The differences between the computer and professional printing can be daunting. The pixels-versus-dots issue is bad enough; but how the computer sees color is different as well. The computer does not see a full-color photograph in terms of CMYK, but in Red (R), Green (G), and Blue (B)—or RGB. Like our own eyes, the computer combines colors differently in order to create multiple colors and tones. Before any photograph can be placed in a desktop publishing program or sent off to a printer, it must first be converted to CMYK in Photoshop. This conversion takes place after any and all photo manipulation is complete.

BLACK-AND-WHITE PHOTOGRAPHS

From time to time, you will see black-and-white photographs used in magazine ads. These photographs must be turned into halftones, just as in newspaper. However, the line screen would be 133 rather than 65 or 85.

Why use black-and-white photos when you can use color? Well, one reason is price. It is much cheaper to use a black-and-white photograph than a color photograph. Another reason is that a black-and-white photograph stands out against a lot of color. This independence in appearance attracts readers' attention.

Black-and-white photographs are also excellent mood or attitude setters. Issues such as drinking and driving and the results from such behavior are often difficult to take in color. Sadness or isolation, even the passing of time, can be represented best in black and white—especially with all the bright colors on adjacent pages.

Some products or services, like charities, would not wish to look to affluent or wasteful when soliciting donations. They might prefer black-and-white photography to color.

Fashion ads in black and white are certainly a surprise. They stop the reader, making them spend just a minute longer on this anomaly.

PANTONE MATCHING COLORS

Color choices can include four-color separations (CMYK), or they can be chosen from specific Pantone Matching System (PMS) colors. **PMS colors** are a series of colored chips that have been assigned a number; they are separated by whether they are coated (C) or uncoated (U) colors. A PMS chip book can be found in any art department. These chips and/or numbers accompany an ad to the printer. Choice of coated or uncoated is determined by the paper stock on which you will be printing. It is important to choose the right coated or uncoated label, because a PMS color will change in intensity depending on paper saturation levels. Colors on un-coated papers will be darker than those on coated stocks. So a designer must choose accordingly, making sure color matches are consistent from piece to piece, no matter the paper stock.

The addition of a PMS color is expensive. If you think about each color as being a tube of paint, each additional color beyond the four pro-cess colors must be purchased separately. CMYK can reproduce all colors very closely, but not exactly. If you want an exact kelly green, you'll have to order an additional tube of paint, creating a five-color print job. PMS colors are used to add another specific color beyond those found in four-color photographs. They are often used as graphic accents or in logos.

Spot Color

When black-and-white photographs feature a spot of color, the result is referred to as **spot color.** This is an excellent way to highlight the product by making it stand out in stark contrast to the rest of the photograph. Spot color can give a visual the illusion of three-dimensionality. By adding a spot of color to the photograph, the designer can control eye flow, drawing the viewer's eye directly to the product. Cost depends on the kind of color added to the photograph. Options include a four-color spot or a color cho-sen from the PMS palette.

Duotones

More often used in newspaper, a duotone gives a black-and-white photo-graph a wash of a second color. If you have chosen to design with a black-and-white photograph, you may want a look that spot color cannot achieve. By adding a wash of color, you can give the ad a bit more eye appeal. If you're trying to get an aged or charred appeal with brown, it would be a great time to consider using a duotone.

The choice to use photographs, especially four-color photographs, is expensive. However, color photography at any level—as with duotones or spot color—is worth the price. It brings an ad alive and helps to create interest and involvement from the consumer.

The Appeal of Illustrations

Photographers capture reality; you choose your photographer based on experience in one or more categories such as product specialization, creativity, and even price. Illustrators are chosen based on style. If you are looking for a nostalgic, homey look, you might choose an illustrator with a Norman Rockwell style. If your concept calls for a more modern approach, you may look for someone who uses a Peter Max or Andy Warhol style.

Illustrations can create a mood or trend as easily as a photograph does. Depending on the style and color usage, they can represent a laid-back or upbeat approach.

Bleed is still a critical consideration during the design process. As in a photo shoot, the illustrator needs to know if bleed is required so she can include it during the creation stage.

How do you learn about all these different illustration styles? Many of the most successful illustrators will have a representative. These "reps" stop by the agency from time to time, showing off various artists' works. Other illustrators drop by personally or send out postcards that promote their various styles.

Art directors will also use *Illustrator Annuals* to find the artistic style they are looking for. These annuals are large four-color books that agencies subscribe to. Artists pay to have their work and contact information printed in one or more volumes. Art directors store these annuals for later reference.

As always, deciding whether to use an illustration or a photograph depends on concept. For anything that features customer services, emotional appeals, or any food product, consider photographs. To create personality, think illustration. For ambiance, it's a toss-up. One thing is for sure; illustrations and graphics are less expensive design options than a four-color photograph.

THE ENERGY IN GRAPHICS

Graphics have great potential in magazines. If your product is youthful or modern, consider using a more upbeat or graphic approach.

Graphic design looks at life and situations abstractly. Bright colors and multiple shapes, both geometric and organic, are used to create modern and bold designs. These shapes when used together are often disjointed, and they are used to create an alternative view of life. If set off by a lot of white space, this design style screams off the page, especially if other advertising in the magazine is using traditional photography.

Graphics can also be as simple as a divider line between columns of copy, or a graphic bar such as those used in a Mondrian layout style.

Graphic design is very bold since it often employs flat colors rather than tonal qualities. Designers choose colors that are vibrant and that often have symbolic meaning.

Screen Tints

PMS colors also allow for the use of screen tints. A PMS color is 100 percent of color, or the original color. Screen tints are an inexpensive addition to any design, and they can give a two- or three-color job more depth without the need to purchase another tube of paint. Created photographically, each tint used gives the appearance of a new color. A 10-percent screen of royal blue, for example, will look baby blue.

Color by the Numbers

The number of colors that appear in an ad affects cost. Depending on the client's budget, a designer can choose from a number of color options. The simplest and most inexpensive is a one-color job. Here an ad prints in only one color, such as a black-and-white newspaper ad. It is important to note that in printing, white is not a color. Purchasing a tube of white paint would be redundant, since your paper is white.

Using two colors is another option. This would be any two-color combination. Just remember that type is easiest to read in a dark color; so usually one of the colors is black, navy, brown, forest green, and so on.

Beyond the two-color combination is a three-color job, made up of any combination of three colors, as well as a four-color job that includes none of the CMYK choices.

The Mood of Color

Effective color choices can be used as design elements. Certain colors create specific emotions and can be used to set a mood or attract the eye. Color is also easier to remember than product names.

The Meaning of Color

Color can make us feel warm, cold, stressed, or lethargic. We know the sun should be yellow and the sky blue. The elegance, reassurance, or casualness of a color comes from life's experiences; we see life in color and use it to describe an event, an emotion, the passage of time, or life and death.

When using color, be sure it does not compete with other colors on the page but complements the mood you are trying to attain. Elegance is portrayed with more white than color; red and yellow are hot; blue is cool and green life. So be careful you don't use too much color, or the ad may become stressful or gaudy-looking to readers.

The Placement of Color

Text should be the darkest color on the page, unless you're creating a reverse. If you are going to place text on a colored background, be sure the background is light enough and the text bold enough to maintain good readability. Serif type in small point sizes can break up and should not be placed on a colored background.

Reverses in design create a focal point. Add a little color and they take on a personality. Any dark-colored background can be used, so long as it creates enough contrast to offset the text. Reverse text need not be white, but any light color.

WHEN TO USE A BORDER

Borders or frames are considered graphic additions. You can't use a border on a full-page magazine ad, due to problems associated with the trimming; you can, however, use a decorative frame. Creating white space around an ad pulls the viewer in and creates a cozy members-only atmosphere. Using a light-colored background that bleeds beyond the border creates an open, airy feel.

LAYOUT OPTIONS

Magazine sizes differ, and so do ad sizes. The most common full-page magazine size is 8½ × 11 inches. There are larger magazines, like *Life,* as well as smaller ones, like *National Geographic.* Size is definitely not an indication of quality in magazine design.

The most standard ad sizes are one-third page, one-fourth page, one-half page, two-thirds page, and full page (or 8½ × 11). You also have the option to use two-page ads or double-page spreads.

Left and right page placement needs to be considered during both the design stage and during photo shoots. If you have people, animals, or

This ad shows both a graphic frame and the vertical
use of type.

anything that can gaze in one direction or another, it needs to gaze to the
inside of the magazine.

Traditionally, it is best to have models looking into the page rather
than off. I would consider this a place to start rather than a hard-and-fast
rule. The key to all design rule breaking is to have a point or a justifiable
reason for changing the rules. If you've got one, then anything goes.

Double-page spreads offer new design experiences. Everything can
get bigger, and photographs can get closer. Designing in a horizontal versus vertical format is more difficult, however. Page space must be used
wisely to avoid gaps and unnecessary holes.

Another problem is that a spread has a **gutter.** This is the area that will
be pulled into the binding of the magazine. It is important to be sure
nothing of importance falls into that gutter, whether it is a headline or
photographic detail. You should leave at least one-fourth inch of space on
either side of the gutter. As a beginning designer, I would suggest drawing
the gutter on your layout area so that you do not forget about it and can
design around it.

LET'S FOLD SOMETHING

The type of fold found in magazines is called a **gatefold.** A gatefold can be one or more folds that fold in toward the ad's center when the magazine is closed and can fold out for viewing.

A gatefold can vary in size, but most often is a full-size third panel, one-sixteenth to one-eighth inch smaller than the page size; this allows the magazine to close without rumpling or folding the ad. Another common option is a partial page fold, which can vary in size but is usually around 2.5 inches to 3 inches.

Gatefolds are used not only to extend the ad but also to add grandeur and invoke curiosity. Extending the photograph entices readers to open the panel, involving them in the ad and holding their interest a few minutes longer. Coupons, contests, or sweepstakes information can often be found on or under these smaller folds. Usually small gatefolds overlay the bottom photograph, making it important during printing that registration be exact.

Designers hate added clutter, so delegating it to a side panel is a great alternative that affects the overall design very little. Gatefolds are expensive, so it is important to make sure your client's budget can accommodate this very enticing design addition.

CHAPTER TWELVE

PUTTING THE PIECES IN PLACE

MAGAZINE DEADLINES

Unlike the twenty-four-hour turnaround of most newspapers, magazine deadlines are long. You are not looking at days or weeks, but often months before publication. Putting a magazine issue out is a lengthy process. It takes time to arrange articles and photo shoots, lay out the magazine, fit copy, and print. It is unusual for a magazine ad to be added at the last minute, as is done in newspaper. Since magazines do not promote sales or anything that deals with a tight or limited sales schedule, these extended deadlines are reasonable.

Preparation for a magazine ad could begin six months in advance of the publication date. There is a lot to be done at the ad design stage as well. Concept needs to be developed and approved, photo shoots need to be arranged, and color separations need to be ordered.

GETTING AN AD PRINTED

Printing requires meeting your deadlines. Quality four-color separations need to be done and then color corrected by the designer or design team. Food should look appetizing—not too green or yellow—and models should look healthy, not jaundiced or lobsterlike. Any photo retouching is completed when blemishes, unflattering shadows, or intense or washed-out areas have been removed or corrected.

All ads must be double-checked for size, trim, and bleed and proofed for typos or flipped photographs. All artwork, photographs, and type fonts should be collected and must accompany the ad to the printer or publisher.

SOME NEGATIVES

Negatives associated with magazine design include expense, limited publication opportunities and lengthy deadlines. Any reproduction problems associated with magazines are eliminated due to the use of both better paper and print quality. Young designers will find magazine design a bit more stressful than newspaper design. There is less room for error here, and there are more steps to go through.

SOME POSITIVES

Color is always a positive, though it must be used wisely. PMS colors can be expensive and should be used only when budget and design dictate.

Reproduction issues are another positive. Photographs used in magazines have a smaller dot pattern, allowing for greater detail. Since full-size magazine ads do not require a border, bleed photographs are possible; this allows designers to extend the design area.

More ad copy can be used, sustaining readers' interest long enough to educate; and type can be designed into the product's personality. The highly targeted nature of magazine readers allows copy to speak directly to the person most likely to purchase the product, the person who clearly understands its benefits. "Been there, done that" works great here, as consumers relate their experiences to those the product can solve.

CHAPTER THIRTEEN

DIGITAL PREPRESS

THE COMPUTER

So many student designers want to design on the computer, abandoning brainstorming sessions, thumbnail ideas, and quickly rendered hand-drawn roughs that reflect both good and bad ideas by the tens, twenties, and thirties. On the computer, once you hit the delete key, all ideas good and bad are gone. You have no reference material to work from; this is especially important if you have to start over.

The computer is not a design tool; it's a production tool. Your brain is the design tool, and your eyes are the layout tools. The computer has yet to become an imaginative designer. Its job is to reproduce your good ideas.

A well-designed rough can save hours of computer adjustments. Type that fits within the allotted space, and photos that are properly cropped and show the product's attributes, come from thinking the idea through—not just randomly moving objects around in the window. Once you master design and its infinite options, you can abandon the hand-drawn stage.

An ad being reproduced on the computer should *fit* with little adjustment. Time should not be wasted in adjusting and guessing at the visual outcome. A good guess always means wasted time, and it is a warning bell that your headline or visual will have to be resized, the body copy and layout reworked, or both. Basically, without references, you end up starting over.

SOFTWARE

Quark and PageMaker are the two most popular desktop publishing software programs. Adobe InDesign, the newcomer on the block, is making good progress. To date, most advertising agencies use Quark and Macintosh computers for design. The software program, however, is usually decided for you due to employer or printer preference.

PREPARING YOUR AD FOR THE PRINTER

The process of preparing a magazine ad for printing begins during the design process. Every full-size magazine ad has three main parts a designer must concern himself with—live, trim, and possibly bleed. Since magazine ads do not have a border that determines size, printer's instructions or marks are required.

Every full-size magazine ad has at least a live area and trim. The live area does not receive any production marks, since it has nothing to do with size or preproduction requirements. I would, however, strongly suggest

This example shows trim, bleed, and registration marks.

placing a 7 × 10 inch margin guide inside your ad. This way you will know where type should be confined.

Trim marks can take many forms, but most commonly they are one horizontal and vertical line placed at each of the ad's corners, about a quarter-inch out and a half-inch long. If you were to place a ruler between marks, you would get the trim or ad size.

Bleed is considered present when any visual or graphic extends beyond the trim marks or edges of the page. As mentioned earlier, it is a design option that is not always used.

Registration marks are not a part of the design process, but are required for printing. Registration marks are added to the ad during the desktop publishing stage. They are usually centered and placed on either side of the ad. Like trim marks, they can take many forms; but they are usually a plus sign with a circle. The printer uses these marks to align multiple negatives while printing.

Each photograph and each PMS color or screen tint that appears in your ad will need to have a separate negative shot, or pulled, during print-

This ad uses repetition to feature results.

ing. In the case of four-color photographs or color logos, a full-size negative of each of the CMYK colors will need to be pulled.

For big press jobs, negatives will be reassembled or aligned using the registration marks, and plates will be pulled.

Colors that butt up against each other will need to be trapped. **Trapping** occurs when two different colors touch each other in a design. The darkest color will slightly overlap the lighter color to keep any white space from appearing between colors. This space can occur if negatives, plates, or paper are misaligned—also referred to as being *out of register*. This is a very serious business, because it can affect how the ad looks in print. Trapping is best left to the experts, but it can be done with any desktop publishing software.

COLLECT FOR OUTPUT

Before sending any job to the printer, you'll need to consider a couple of things. The first is how do you send the ad? Small files like those for magazine ads can be sent to the printer on a Zip disk. Larger files—for example, an annual report—can be sent on CD. Superlarge formats will need to be saved on a Jaz disk.

Next you have to make sure all the pieces are attached to the ad. Just because you can see your photographs or fonts on the screen doesn't mean the printer will be able to.

All photographs need to be collected. In your desktop software you will have an option called "Collect for Output." This function will let you know if you have any missing fonts or photographs.

All fonts used in the ad should be sent along to the printer. To send a font, just drag the font suitcase located on your hard drive to your Fonts folder. You can drag the whole font list, or just the typeface(s) used in the ad.

Everything can be salvaged if you send all existing work with your ad. Save each component in a different file folder, to make it easier for your printer to locate specific items. The labeling of file folders should be kept simple; either number them or label them according to the enclosed contents.

File Folder 1:   The completed ad

File Folder 2:   All photographs

File Folder 3:   Your font file

File Folder 4:   Any work done in Illustrator

Place all these folders into one holding folder, or just keep them separate.

Once you have completed each of the above steps, you're ready to send your Zip file or CD to the printer. Send a printout along with your disk or CD. A printout of the final ad allows the printer to preview the ad and helps him to solve any minor problems when he knows what he is looking for.

TROUBLESHOOTING

When you're using the Collect for Output function, two kinds of messages concerning visuals or text will pop up. The first is missing picture or modified picture; the second is missing or modified fonts.

A prompt telling you that you have missing or modified pictures or fonts usually means some change has taken place to the type or the photograph within the desktop publishing software. Most often somebody resized it, renamed it, or placed a drop shadow or outline around it. This is an easy fix since all desktop publishing programs will prompt you through the process.

If you can't print in-house, or are having trouble bringing your photograph(s) into your desktop publishing program, you probably (1) forgot to save your photographs as a TIFF; (2) forgot to flatten your layers in Photoshop; (3) added a drop shadow; or (4) added bold or italic styles to a font that either does not support them or is not installed on your printer.

CHAPTER FOURTEEN

LET'S GIVE IT A TRY

Comfort.

The room should feel just as serene as it looks.

Pier 1

EXERCISE LEVEL ONE: BRAINSTORMING

Independently, work on coming up with three concept pitches for the product or service assigned in class. Choose a unique selling proposition (USP) or big idea, and build your concept ideas around it. Create a word list of 20–25 words to help with the visual/verbal process. Present all your work to the class.

EXERCISE LEVEL TWO: WORD LIST

Don't get caught up in the excitement of one good idea, whether it relates to the USP or big idea or not. Writing out ideas and concepts both visually and verbally helps you not only with understanding your assignment, but with understanding the why of message development. Begin the design process by creating a word list of 20–25 words to get the creative juices flowing for the product presented in class. Then fill out the Think Sheet from chapter 9. Next, present your preliminary ideas to the class, or work in teams and combine ideas. Be able to back up your decisions.

EXERCISE LEVEL THREE: THUMBNAILS

In this exercise, you'll begin looking at visual execution of your word list and Think Sheet. Create twenty thumbnails from your best concept development ideas. Be sure each thumb is different; do not reuse headlines, subheads, typefaces, layout styles, or visuals. Try as many different layout styles as you can. Think of the trade-offs regarding redundancy versus diversity, and offer the client options. Present your thumbnails to the class or instructor. Final rough size: Live: 7 × 10 inches Trim: 8½ × 11 inches.

EXERCISE LEVEL FOUR: ROUGHS

Level four begins the rough stage. Choose three out of your twenty thumbnails that you will take to roughs. These thumbs may have been chosen by you, the class, or the instructor. These roughs should be very polished. Use references for visuals and type if your drawing skills need a little support. Present your three roughs to the class. Live: 7 × 10 inches Trim: 8½ × 11 inches.

CLASS CRITIQUES

Use the Think Sheet that you originally created to evaluate your concept. Hand out copies to the class. How many things had to change and why? What were some of the challenges you encountered? Compare and contrast through discussion with your classmates your successes and ultimate failures.

EVALUATION

Use the Project Evaluation Sheet from chapter 9 for determining success and highlighting areas that still need work. The Project Evaluation Sheet has two important functions. First, it will be used by your instructor or classmates to determine your final grade. Secondly, it should be used by you as a self-evaluation tool to make sure you have successfully completed all aspects of the assignment.

EXERCISE LEVEL FIVE: DESIGN WITH BLEED

For this exercise, begin the whole design process again. This time, create a full-size ad; and be sure to add a bleed component. Present your design to the class.

Live: 7 × 10 inches Trim: 8½ × 11 inches Bleed: Allow one-fourth inches beyond trim.

EXERCISE LEVEL SIX: DIFFERENT APPROACHES, SAME CONCEPT

In exercise level six, you'll begin the whole process again. This time, instead of offering three separate concept ideas for your USP or big idea, present three different approaches for the same concept. Present your approaches to the class. Full-size ad; bleed optional.

EXERCISE LEVEL SEVEN: CO-OP AD

For this exercise, create a co-op ad for two compatible products. The ad should include a coupon or order form that can be used with purchase or for obtaining additional information. Full-size ad; bleed optional.

EXERCISE LEVEL EIGHT: NEWSPAPER AD

For this exercise, create a newspaper ad, 3 columns × 11 inches, that accompanies the concept you chose in level six.

Glossary of Terms

ascender The part of a letterform that extends upward and away from the body of a letter, as with the letters *b* and *d.*

banners An announcement device in the shape of a black or dark-colored bar that is often placed at the top of an ad. These bars can also be used as page dividers featuring either white or a light-colored type.

baseline See **descender.**

big idea A creative solution that sets a product or service off from the competition while at the same time solving a client's advertising problem.

bleed A photograph, illustration, background color, or graphic element that extends beyond the trim size or the size of the ad on one or more sides, leaving no complete outer edge of white space.

body copy The descriptive copy that works to make a sale or create an image. Focus is on copy features such as color, price, and size, and/or features a visual/verbal message.

burst An announcement device that looks like a fireworks explosion; usually a dark color such as black, with type that reverses to white.

callout A small amount of copy that appears alongside or below an individual image, connected by a small line.

CMYK The dots that make up a full-color photograph are composed of concentrated percentages of cyan (C), magenta (M), yellow (Y), and black (K). Combinations of these four colors create all colors found in a color photograph.

column inches The width measurement of a newspaper ad, as determined by the newspaper.

clip art Publicly available line-art drawings that can be used without gaining permission.

cooperative advertising Two individual but compatible clients pair up to share the cost of advertising and to encourage consumers to use their product or services together.

creative brief Also known as a *copy platform;* is developed from the creative strategy and defines the *big idea* or *unique selling proposition.*

The creative brief also looks at the individual product or service's features and benefits, outlines tactics, and redefines the target market.

creative A broad term for the conceptual process and any advertising material that is ultimately produced by *creatives.*

creative concept An idea that imaginatively solves the client's advertising problem.

creatives The team of art directors and copywriters that are involved in the creative activity, especially involving the creation of advertisements.

creative strategy A part of the marketing process. It outlines the creative approach needed to accomplish marketing goals and/or objectives.

cropping The removal of any unnecessary part(s) of a photograph, allowing the designer to dispose of information that is not necessary to the design.

demographics Defines the target market in terms of age, income, sex, marital and professional status, education, number of children, and so forth.

demonstration approach A creative approach that focuses on comparing the client's product to the competition.

descender The part of the letterform that projects downward below the *baseline* (the imaginary line that type sits on), as with the letters *g* or *p.*

detail copy Small copy that features addresses, phone numbers, web addresses, credit card information, e-mail addresses, store hours, parking, and so on.

duotone An additional color added to a black-and-white photograph adding depth, creating a faux full-color feel.

educational approach A creative approach that is used when a product or service is in the news or has some kind of educational value to the consumer.

emotional approach A creative approach that focuses on a consumer's needs and wants. Facts about a product/service are not as important as the image and personal satisfaction the product/service will bring.

endorsement approach A creative approach that uses an announcer or celebrity who does not personally use the product or service and is being paid for his or her time.

eyeballing Refers to what type looks like after manual adjustments are made to line spacing or letterspacing.

factual approach A creative approach designed around the facts associated with a product or service.

feature approach   A creative approach that focuses on one major feature of a product or service.

focus group   The gathering together of a representative sample of the target market to use or try the product in a controlled environment.

font   A complete catalog of uppercase and lowercase letters, numbers, and punctuation in a specific typeface and style. Fonts can be roman, italic, boldface, condensed, and so on. See also **typeface.**

four-color photograph   The four-color dot pattern, composed of *CMYK,* needed to reproduce a color photograph or illustration.

freestanding inserts   Also known as *supplemental advertising;* full-color ads that are inserted into the newspaper, usually featuring coupons and/or to announce special sales or promotions.

gatefold   One or more foldouts found in magazines that fold in toward the ad's center when the magazine is closed and can fold out for viewing.

geographics   Another way to break down the target market, by looking at where a person lives.

graphics   Additional devices such as grids, bars, and boxes that add dimension and/or organization to an ad. Other types of graphics include dashed lines (for coupons), arrows, snipes, bursts, and even type.

greeking   A haphazard arrangement of letters, numbers, punctuation, and paragraph breaks; used to temporarily represent body copy.

gutter   A white space created by the inner margins of two facing pages of a magazine or book. Some of this area is used in the binding.

headline   The largest copy in an ad. Focus is on highlighting the ad's *unique selling proposition* (USP) or *big idea.*

halftone   The name given a black-and-white photograph that has been converted to a dot pattern.

humorous approach   A creative approach that focuses on placing the product or service and/or the target in an unusual or outrageous situation in which the product/service solves a problem.

instructional approach   A creative approach that focuses on teaching the consumer how to do something or how a product or service can solve a problem.

kerning   The removal or addition of space between letters on the computer. A numerical value, most often a negative one, is given to the space between letters.

leading   Leading (rhymes with "heading") is a computer term that gives a specific numerical value (measured in *points*) to the amount of white space appearing between lines of text.

legibility   An ad's message that can be easily understood when viewed quickly.

line screens   The size of the dot pattern needed to reproduce a photograph in any print media, measured in lines per inch (lpi).

line spacing   In design, this term refers to the amount of white space showing between lines of text.

live area   The area where type is confined. Any kind of visual or graphic can extend beyond this area. The live area protects elements from being cut off when the magazine is trimmed.

logo   A company or product's symbol.

margin   The white space that appears between the inside edges of an ad and where the copy or visual elements begin. Margins can be almost any size, but they should be no less than one-fourth inch on all four sides.

marketing plan   A client's business plan. It outlines the company's strengths and weaknesses as well as the opportunities and threats affecting the product or service. It determines marketing objectives, profiles the marketing strategy, and looks at budget issues and evaluation tactics.

news event   See **educational approach.**

orphan   A short line that appears at the bottom of a page, or a word (or part of a word) on a line by itself at the end of a paragraph.

Pantone Matching System (PMS)   A series of colored chips that have been assigned a number and are separated by whether they are coated (C) or uncoated (U) colors.

pixels   A series of small colored or gray-tinted squares that create a photo's image and/or color variations on a computer screen.

point   The basic unit of type measurement, determined by the height of a typeface's capital letters.

printing plate   Used in printing. A thin, flexible metal sheet with the ad's image etched into the surface.

process color photograph   See **four-color photograph.**

psychographics   Breaks the target market down by looking at lifestyle, or how the target lives.

qualitative data   Information gathered by using open-ended questions that can be distributed and collected through interviews, convenience polling, or focus groups.

quantitative data   Information gathered by using closed-ended or controlled surveys, where participants must choose their answers from a preselected set of responses.

readability   The ease with which an ad can be easily read at a glance.

registration marks   Used to align negatives while printing.

reminder approach   A creative approach that focuses on reminding the consumer about well-known products or services.

resolution   The size of the pixel needed to reproduce an image on the computer screen.

retail advertising   Another term used for newspaper advertising.

roughs   Also known as *layouts;* these are full-size representations of the final piece, with all elements in place and tightly rendered in black and white or color. Conceptual devices such as headlines, subheads, and visuals are readable and viewable.

sans serif   A typeface design that is unadorned, having no feet or appendages. See also **serif.**

screen tints   Tonal areas that can be used as highlights or shadows. Tones range from very light to medium to dark to very dark and are created from any solid color. Known as *shades* in desktop publishing.

serif   A typeface design that features feet or delicate appendages that protrude from the edges of the letters and other characters.

slogan   A statement that represents the company's philosophy, or a product or service's image; the slogan is usually placed above or below the logo.

snipe   A triangle-shaped announcement device, usually placed in one of the top corners of an ad. Usually a dark color such as black, with type that reverses to white.

spot color   Black-and-white photographs that feature a spot of color.

stock art   Existing photographs of all varieties that can be purchased and used in an ad.

subhead   A secondary heading that explains the main headline's message further. Should entice the reader into the body copy.

super comprehensives   Also known as *super comps;* these are created from your final roughs. They are generated on the computer with all headlines, subheads, visuals, a logo, and—for the first time—completed body copy in place, simulating exactly how the finished design will look and read.

superiors   Numbers or symbols such as dollar or cent signs that are set at least half the size of the listed price.

target market   The group of individuals that have been determined most likely to buy your product or use your service.

teaser approach   A creative approach that focuses on building curiosity for new or improved products or services, often without showing the product.

testimonial approach   A creative approach that uses a celebrity or common man on the street to endorse a product/service by telling about their personal experiences with the product/service.

thumbnails   Small, proportionate drawings that are used to place concept ideas on paper.

trapping   Occurs when two different colors touch each other in a design. The darkest color will slightly overlap the lighter color to keep any white space from appearing between colors when printing.

trim size   The full size of the magazine page, including margins. *Trim* is also used when referring to the full size of an ad. *Trim marks* indicate where the ad or magazine will be trimmed during production.

typeface   A collection of fonts with a specific design and name, such as Times Roman. See also **font.**

type style   Refers to the form of the typeface used, for example, boldface, italic, roman, and serif or sans serif.

type weight   Refers to the thickness or thinness of the typeface's body.

unique selling proposition (USP)   A creative solution that promotes a product feature as unique, setting it off from the competition.

visual   Basic design element; can take the form of a photograph, an illustration, line art, or graphic design.

widow   A single word or a short line that appears at the top of a page or at the top of a new column of copy.

Bibliography

Assadi, Barbara, and Galen Gruman. *QuarkXPress 6 for Dummies.* Hoboken, N.J.: Wiley.

Book, Albert C., and Dennis C. Schick. *Fundamentals of Copy & Layout: Everything You Need to Know to Prepare Better Ads.* 3rd ed. Lincolnwood, Ill.: National Textbook Company, 1984.

Duncan, Tom. *IMC: Using Advertising & Promotion to Build Brands.* New York: McGraw-Hill Irwin, 2002.

Nelson, Roy Paul. *The Design of Advertising.* 2nd & 6th ed. Dubuque, Iowa: Wm. C. Brown, 1973, 1989.

Swann, Alan. *Graphic Design School: A Foundation Course in the Principles and Practices of Graphic Design.* New York: Van Nostrand Reinhold, 1991.

———. *How to Understand and Use Design and Layout.* Cincinnati, Ohio: North Light Books, 1997.

Vanden Bergh, Bruce, and Helen Katz. *Advertising Principles: Choice, Challenge, Change.* Lincolnwood, Ill.: NTC Publishing Group, 1999.

Weinmann, Elaine, and Peter Lourekas. *Visual Quickstart Guide: QuarkXPress for Windows & Macintosh.* Berkeley, Calif.: Peachpit Press, 2004.

Wong, Wucius. *Principles of Two-Dimensional Design.* New York: Van Nostrand Reinhold, 1972.

———. *Principles of Form and Design.* New York: Van Nostrand Reinhold, 1993.

Zelanski, Paul, and Mary Pat Fisher. *Design Principles and Problems.* New York: Holt, Rinehart and Winston, 1984.

Index

ABOUT THE AUTHOR

Robyn Blakeman received her bachelor's degree from the University of Nebraska in 1980 and her master's degree from Southern Methodist University in Dallas, Texas, in 1996.

Professor Blakeman began teaching advertising and graphic design in 1987 with the Art Institutes. As an assistant professor of advertising, she taught both graphic and computer design at Southern Methodist University. While at West Virginia University, Professor Blakeman held several positions, including advertising program chair, coordinator of the integrated marketing communications online graduate certificate program, and coordinator of student affairs and curriculum, in addition to developing the creative track in layout and design. She was responsible for designing and developing the first online integrated marketing communications graduate certificate and online integrated marketing communications graduate programs in the country.

In the years 2002 and 2004, Professor Blakeman was nominated for inclusion in *Who's Who among America's Teachers*. She was included in *Who's Who in America* in 2003, has received the Kappa Tau Alpha honorary from her peers, and was voted journalism professor of the year for 2001–2002.

She is the author of the upcoming book, *Creative Strategy for Integrated Marketing Communications,* and currently teaches design at the University of Tennessee.

CREDITS

Kristie Abraham's work appears on page 86.*

Joanne Asztalos's work appears on pages 91 and 167.

Justin Barker's work appears on pages 130 and 137.

Margaux Byrne's work appears on pages 8 and 161.

Anna Camele's work appears on page 54.

Jessica Carpenter's work appears on page 139.

Derek Channell's work appears on pages 29 (bottom) and 127.

Jason Coffman's work appears on pages 115 and 147.

Joe Davich's work appears on page 30 (top).

Jennifer Donahue's work appears on page 24.

Heather Elmes's work appears on page 132 and 135.

Todd Goettelmann's work appears on page 107.

Larae Greer's work appears on page 154.

Mary Beth Held's work appears on pages 1, 85, 99, 144, and 145.

Jennifer Holstine's work appears on pages 49, 63, and 138.

Amanda Honce's work appears on pages 12, 37, 48, 60, 65, 66, 68, 95, 103, 113, and 142 (top).

Lorrie Jackula's work appears on pages 30 (bottom), 32, 96, 105, 106, and 143.

Rebecca Kindig's work appears on page 164.

Matt Lehosit's work appears on page 31.

Crystal Lewis's work appears on page 44.

Leslie Linton's work appears on page 47.

Sam Maddox's work appears on page 25.

Tiffany Mailen's work as a student at the University of Tennessee appears on page 59.

Stephen Murray's work appears on page 140.

Barbara Noonan's work appears on page 100.

Katie Noonan's work appears on pages 16, 22, 36, 58 (both), 64 (top), 67, 71, 104, 133, 142 (bottom), and 157.

Stacy Pachuta's work appears on page 23.

Julie Pikel's work appears on pages 101 and 146.

*All work created while studying at West Virginia University unless otherwise indicated.

183

Tawnya Stanford's work appears on pages 11 and 50.
Nick Taylor's work appears on pages 52 and121.
Bradley Tennant's work appears on page 43.
Andrea Vanin's work appears on page 53.
Chris Vaughan's work appears on pages 19, 28, and 29 (top).
Susan Wooley's work appears on pages 27 and 116.

Breinigsville, PA USA
11 October 2010
247136BV00003B/1/P